I hop
my book and
my it show you
the power
you have to
change the
world 1 spark
at a time

Love
Daniel A2J

HOW TO CHANGE YOUR PICKLES AND ANCHORS INTO KEYS!

DAVID L. HILL

ONE SPARK FOUNDATION

WESTBOW
PRESS®
A DIVISION OF THOMAS NELSON
& ZONDERVAN

Scriptures taken from the Holy Bible, New International Version®, NIV®. Copyright © 1973, 1978, 1984, 2011 by Biblica, Inc.™ Used by permission of Zondervan. All rights reserved worldwide. www.zondervan.com The "NIV" and "New International Version" are trademarks registered in the United States Patent and Trademark Office by Biblica, Inc.

This book is a work of non-fiction. Unless otherwise noted, the author and the publisher make no explicit guarantees as to the accuracy of the information contained in this book and in some cases, names of people and places have been altered to protect their privacy.

WestBow Press books may be ordered through booksellers or by contacting:

WestBow Press
A Division of Thomas Nelson & Zondervan
1663 Liberty Drive
Bloomington, IN 47403
www.westbowpress.com
1 (866) 928-1240

Because of the dynamic nature of the Internet, any web addresses or links contained in this book may have changed since publication and may no longer be valid. The views expressed in this work are solely those of the author and do not necessarily reflect the views of the publisher, and the publisher hereby disclaims any responsibility for them.

Any people depicted in stock imagery provided by Getty Images are models, and such images are being used for illustrative purposes only. Certain stock imagery © Getty Images.

ISBN: 978-1-9736-4281-7 (sc)
ISBN: 978-1-9736-4280-0 (hc)
ISBN: 978-1-9736-4282-4 (e)

Library of Congress Control Number: 2018912280

Print information available on the last page.

WestBow Press rev. date: 11/15/2018

Dedication

First and foremost I want to thank God for always being there for me, even when I thought He was not. I thank Him for showing me how to change my pickles and anchors into keys.

I want to thank my wife who has put up with me and loved me, even when I was not loving myself.

She has been my rock, through everything that I have been through.

Contents

Foreword

In the summer of 1973 my mother met a boy, and a few weeks later she found out she was pregnant. They stuck together, but a few misplaced words resulted in a split shortly before I came along. I was born in April of 1974.

When I was four months old, my mom met the man that I would know as dad. It wasn't long until he had moved in. He partied all night, slept all day, and never worked, while my mom held a job and supported us. He was a regular drug user, and now so was my mom. Drunken drug-filled nights turned into fights and beatings for mom.

The drug habit had progressed and now my parents were full-blown drug dealers. One thing had not changed—the drunken, drug-filled evenings regularly ended in fights and beatings. As I grew older, the rage started being taken out on me. The measurement to know when I had had enough was when the thin wide board broke. I lived in a deep depression in those years, which caused me to not perform in school; I had few friends and lived in constant fear. Lack of performance in school resulted in more violence at home and the vicious cycle continued. I remember wishing I could just die.

When I was five years old, we moved to southeast Florida. The next few years were some of the darkest years of my life. In Florida, new drugs were introduced and the violence became much worse. My mother attempted suicide three times. I found her two of those times, and I was never allowed to call for help. He always got her back, once by biting her ear in half and then stitching it up himself with dental floss and a sewing needle.

Our life of secrecy that resulted from the drug dealing meant I could never have friends over and I couldn't participate in the typical activities like sports, Boy Scouts, etc. When I was seven, I convinced my mom to let me play little league baseball. My dad said that I wouldn't be any good at it and it was a waste of time and money. Well, I went to every practice, and while I had no idea how to play, I was so excited and knew I could learn. Finally, the first game came and I was so eager. My coach said I was doing well and I begged my mom and dad to come. They did! Unfortunately, dad was drunk and high when he arrived. I got up to bat for the first time ever and struck out. I was disappointed, but the worst part was the swearing and name calling—from my dad. He marched onto the field, grabbed me by the ear, and drug me off, telling me how I was not going to embarrass him any more than I already had. When I got home, he threatened me with the bat I had just failed him with. My mom intervened, which resulted in a beating for her. I remember getting a board and breaking it over his back to get him off her. That resulted in fifteen stitches for me. We left that time—for a long time.

When my mom and I attempted to leave him (after repeated beatings), my dad continually begged for forgiveness, promising change. He showered us with gifts and treated us as though we were the most important things in his life. He would tell me how much he loved me and how I meant the world to him. We always ended up going back for more.

Beatings occurred on a regular basis until I was eight. My mom was pregnant and they agreed to back off on the drug use—and so the violence subsided. Once his son was born, I was never introduced as his son again. I was now referred to as "her white kid." He once told me that I wasn't even his child and I was lucky he even let me live there. Six months later mom was pregnant again, and this time it was a girl. He treated "his kids" like royalty. If I made any mistake, especially if one of them got hurt, the beatings were worse than ever.

When I was ten, mom left him and we returned to Wichita and lived with family. Before long he followed us and convinced mom to give him one more chance. No more drugs and no more drinking was the promise. They just had to do a few more deals to get some money together to pay off debts and get a fresh start.

One night in the summer of 1985 I went to sleep and was woken the next morning by being drug out of bed by my hair. It was about 5:30 AM and my mom had gone out to do a drug deal the night before. All my dad knew was that she hadn't come home, but the truth was she had been arrested. He punched me repeatedly, demanding that I tell him where my mother was. Then he took me to the front porch and threw me on top of my bike, cutting my side open. I was bleeding badly, but he didn't care. Glaring at me, he said, "Get on that bike and go find your mother. If you don't come back, you'll never see your brother and sister again!"

I rode down the street early in the morning in my underwear—bleeding. I went to my aunt's house, which was about a mile away. There I found both my grandparents and my aunt in tears. Mom had called them and they knew what had happened. The deal the night before was a setup. They took me inside, cleaned me up, and gave me some clothes. Just minutes later, my dad showed up, demanding that I leave with him. My grandpa met him in the yard with his rifle, told him that he didn't have any legal claim to me, and made him unload my brother and sister from the car.

Later in the day my mom called him and told him what had happened. She told him they wanted her to turn him in and she could go free. She, of course, protected him and he promised he was done for good—no more drugs at all. He assured her that he was going to take care of the kids while she was away and build a home for her to return to. She agreed.

Ten days later, he was arrested in an airport with $10K worth of cocaine strapped to his legs. We were left with our aunt, while both parents were sentenced to prison. Visiting my mom in prison was a terrible experience. During this time, my aunt encouraged me to make friends and get involved. I joined the Boy Scouts and one of the leaders there took me under his wing. He used to take me out to lunch and started taking me to church. There I found out that there was a God that loved me even though I felt so worthless and ashamed. That was the beginning for me.

I remember walking in on a conversation while visiting my other aunt's house outside of town. I heard her say, "I hate to see what he is going to turn out like." I looked her in the eye and said, "Just watch; I'm going to do something great." She didn't mean anything by what she said. Any of us probably would have had the same expectation based on the life I had led. I took it as a challenge. I knew that with God in my life, I could do great things and make a difference.

Eighteen months later, mom was released and went to mandatory drug rehab. When she completed that, she came home promising that things would be different. Mom, too, had experienced the love that God had for her and she planned to live her life in service to the Lord moving forward. When she came home she didn't drink or do drugs, but she was very bitter and angry. Life was hard for a convicted felon, and raising three kids alone didn't help. The beatings began again, but this time mom was the one handing them out. They were less frequent but just as violent. It seemed I couldn't do anything right and, once again, I felt helpless.

When I was twelve, my friend from the Boy Scout troop got married and moved away. He introduced me to another young man who was a leader, and I started getting to know him. After several months of being friends, he told me he wanted me to get serious about getting through the ranks and working toward my Eagle Scout rank. He came to my house that summer to work on my Physical Fitness merit badge test. It turns out that his version of that merit badge was to help me become familiar with his body. He spent the better part of an afternoon molesting me. Then as he left, he told me I passed the badge and that if I told anyone about what had happened, he would take the badge back and I would be in trouble. I believed this because I was always in trouble. I didn't tell my mom because I just knew it would be my fault, and I felt that it would be more than she could handle.

At the age of fourteen, I went to play basketball with a bunch of guys, and one of them was my teacher. I had a 10 PM curfew, but when we were preparing to go home, one of the cars broke down and they had to use the other one to shuttle everyone home. I was twenty-two minutes late. My teacher came to the house and apologized to my mom. She explained the situation and my mother replied, "It's no big deal." I began to get ready for bed, and after about fifteen minutes she came in with the belt in her hand. She started hitting me. Then, finally, she stopped and began yelling at me. She was slapping me, while telling me how inconsiderate and ungrateful I was and that her whole life would have been different if she hadn't had me. I remember seeing the first lights of daylight before she stopped beating me and screaming at me. Then she told me to get dressed and go to school.

When I arrived at school, the teacher from the night before looked horrified. He took me aside and said he was calling the police. I begged him not to. He called my grandparents who came and picked me up. I went to my grandparent's house where they tended to the open wounds left from the repeated belt strikes on my back and neck. I slept all day, and they took me back to school so my mom could pick me up. I went home and was grounded for two weeks. I was not allowed to leave my room except for school.

That summer I got a job through a low-income program working for the Parks and Recreation Department. After several weeks, I had become acquainted with my supervisor. He was a big muscle-bound man with an IROC Z sports car. He even let me drive his car to Quik Trip on our breaks. I thought I had a real friend. One day, we were in a store room together taking a break. I was sitting on some bags of chalk and he came and sat next to me. He started rubbing my legs and chest, telling me I should go to the gym with him because I had the perfect build to have a great body if I worked out. It made me very uncomfortable and I jumped up and left the room. I avoided him the rest of the day. I didn't say anything about it when I got home.

The next day, I reluctantly went to work and tried to avoid being alone with him again. Then he called me into a bigger store room. I went in like nothing had happened. Again he got very close to me and started touching me. When I tried to pull away, he pushed me down and tore my shorts open. He then exposed himself and got on top of me. I fought him with everything I could. He grabbed an old rake with a splintered handle and told me something was going inside me; it could be him or the rake handle. He raped me! Again, I went home and cleaned up, but I didn't tell my mom what had happened because I was afraid of her response.

The next day, I went in early and went to the other side of the park with one of the other adult employees. He kept asking me if I was okay and I just stayed quiet. Then, at about 7:15, a voice came over the radio, asking if I was on the property. My eyes welled up with tears and he knew something was wrong. The guy I was with began by responding that I was with him. He told the voice on the radio I was helping him and he would send me over in a minute. The response was, "I need him over here now." I begged, "Please don't make me go with him." Thank God, he followed his gut and put me in his truck and took me downtown. There I only told them about him touching me inappropriately. I never mentioned the rape because I was terrified of what my mom would say. I was relocated to another park and he was suspended for two weeks. My mother was called and, surprisingly, she was quite supportive, but if she had known the full story, I am confident she wouldn't have been able to handle it. I bled for three months as I tried to manage my own recovery.

Shortly after this incident, my dad was released from prison. He came back to Wichita and after a few months my mom agreed to take him back. He moved in and he too had built a relationship with the Lord in prison but it was very insincere, and he quickly began drinking and using drugs again. One evening, he and a friend took me to a small dive bar. I was a very tall and fairly well-developed boy, which made me look older than I was. The waitress served us all without question. Then she began to hit on me and as the evening went on, my dad encouraged it. At that time, I was very active in church and had not been sexually active. I didn't drink or smoke. I was a good kid, but I was very insecure and I had no confidence.

Out of the blue my dad said to me, "You should go hit that," and started teasing me about it. He insisted, "She wants you bad!" I told him I wasn't going to do that. This made him angry. He looked at me and said, "Maybe we should go find your boyfriend from the park then. Maybe that's what you want!" Everything suddenly turned red. I was so mad that he would say that, I made a terrible decision. I approached the waitress and was not very gentlemanly about my proposition. My father followed me out of the bar and asked, "Why are you mad? She's hot, and I was just trying to build your confidence." I didn't even respond. I was fifteen, drunk, and had just made a huge mistake. When I arrived home, my mom and dad started fighting. He insisted he was just hanging out with his son. Then he started in on me. Well—I wasn't a little kid anymore—I was both taller and bigger than him. He pushed me against the wall and I belted him. I never told my mom about the bar. She was mad at me and grounded me for being a "punk teenager."

He had accomplished one thing. I did have more confidence; unfortunately, my confidence was all in my pants. I became very sexually active after that and became less engaged in church and growing in my relationship with God. I used as many girls as I needed to so that I could keep feeling good about myself.

The next summer, I went to a church youth camp with some friends. My goal was to nail a few hotties while we were there unsupervised. Little did I know that I would hear a sermon that changed my life. The sermon was called "Daddy God." The preacher spoke of God's love for us and how he loves us more than people can even love their own children. He talked about how we should see ourselves the way God sees us and how God could take away all of the hurt and scars that our lives have left. My life changed that night. I was a different man and I had real confidence. I stopped sleeping around and re-engaged in church. My family had a falling out with our church leadership and, for the most part, walked away from their relationships with the Lord. However, I knew that, without God, I was nothing. I continued to attend a different church on my own. I moved out on my own at seventeen and have dedicated my life to being better than what I had lived.

Since that time, I have dedicated my life to helping people whenever I could. I now have a wonderful wife and three amazing children. I have reconnected with my real father; my stepdad passed away from an assumed overdose a few years ago. I have a successful career, and I oversee a ministry in my church that is aimed at helping families with food, rent, utilities, etc. I try to do something every day to help others and to be an example of God's love. I fail daily, too, but I keep getting back up and going forward and trying to live a life pleasing to God and aware of all He has done for me.

My goal is to impact as many lives as I can and help others who experience some of the things that I went through. I have heard of many who had lives that were worse than mine, but no child should ever experience these kinds of things. No matter what has happened—God can get you through it.

In the last several years, I have become acquainted with Dave Hill and The One Spark Foundation. In all honesty, I watched from a distance before really engaging Dave. I wanted to see if this was all for real. He is a man who has truly dedicated his life to improving the world we live in. Prior to this book, Dave had already made a lasting impact on the world. Few people really achieve that. All you must do is walk down the street with him and you will witness that he practices what he preaches. I am a better man for having seen his example.

Challenges are part of life, but some of us have had more than our fair share of trials. Dave calls these challenges "pickles and anchors." What a perfect analogy for the things in life that can hold us back. The question is: Do you let your circumstances define you or do you let your choices define you?

When I was asked to review this book, I was not prepared for how powerful it was going to be. I was supposed to be taking notes and making comments, but I couldn't stop reading. I was completely captivated by the stories. I read it through and started again before I could make any kind of comment. Every story touched me, and I could relate to each person in some way. What a comfort to feel that so many people have gone through the fire—just like me—and come out on the other side as overcomers. Many were able to overcome because of the One Spark Foundation and Dave's commitment to helping others.

My story is one of emotional, physical, and sexual abuse. Nobody expected anything from me except failure. BUT through the grace of God, a relationship with Jesus Christ, and the support of loving friends and family, I overcame. I have a wonderful wife, three amazing children, as well as a great career. Now, I spend my life trying to help others.

This book takes us on an incredible journey through the lives of many who made the choice to overcome. The stories shared show us all that we can overcome and make a life that is better than the hand we have been dealt. We can be victorious over our pickles and anchors, and we can come out on the other side and make a real difference in the lives of others.

Revelation 12:11 says, "And they have conquered him by the blood of the Lamb and by the word of their testimony, for they loved not their lives unto death." That means that with our Lord Jesus Christ and by sharing our stories, we can defeat the enemy and be overcomers of our obstacles if we put Him first.

Not only can our own lives be impacted, we can also influence the lives of others. Share your story, commit to one small act of kindness (a Spark) each day, and find your way to make a difference. Find a way to share just one Spark.

Dave Hill is the founder of the One Spark Foundation. Its mission is to encourage people to do something (anything!) to make a difference in the world and then to pass it on. Imagine the impact if we all just did one small act to help someone else each day. It would literally change our society as we know it.

It only takes "One Spark" to start a fire that can spread throughout the entire world.

J. Turner
October 2017
Wichita, KS

Introduction

I was having a hard time writing the introduction for this book, because it felt like bragging. I stewed and pondered about how to word it or who I might find to write it for me.

From my bookshelf recently I retrieved a book given to me by my grandmother. It was the first edition of *How to Win Friends and Influence People* by Dale Carnegie. I figured reading a few pages from the book would provide me with some inspiration. When I opened up the book, a letter written by my grandmother fell out.

She had written the letter to me when I was nineteen, so that would be almost thirty-six years ago. Once I read the letter I knew that I had the introduction for *How to Change Your Pickles and Anchors into Keys!*

For the first time in my life, I had a hero and north star who loved me just the way I was. My grandmother lived to be ninety-nine years old. Her nickname was Annie Oakley because she loved her birds and fed them every day. If a cat came along and tried to nab one of her birds, a BB would be firmly implanted in its bottom. She had lots of practice keeping the cats away from her birds. I can remember asking her what she wanted for Christmas when I was in college. She told me she needed a new BB gun so that she could protect her birds.

My grandmother was a woman of prayer, and when she prayed, "God, do whatever it takes to bring him back into the fold," you knew you were in trouble. In 1982, I can remember her advising me against buying a new Trans Am—because it was going to get me into trouble with the girls. She called it the streetwalker car.

She repeatedly told me that the car had to go because God did not want me to be driving a streetwalker car. I did not listen, and the car was where I eventually did get a girl pregnant. Soon after that, headlights mysteriously flashed, windows rolled down by themselves, and the horn went off. This continued until the day the Pontiac folks bought the vehicle back from me because they could not figure out what was wrong with the car and got tired of Granny saying, "God, do whatever it takes to get them to buy back the car." They laughed at first. Every time she said it, you could hear a little fear in their voices.

My Granny loved me, even when I did not love myself.

I hope you enjoy the letter my Granny wrote me.

One last thing—before you read her words—she always called me boy, and one day I asked her why she called me boy instead of my name. She told me it was because I was her boy, her most prized gift from God!

My Granny woke up every morning to a cup of tea, an hour in the Bible, and an hour of prayer. She always told me that when the time came for her to draw her last breath, God would allow her to have her tea, to pray, and read the Bible. When we found her, her tea was gone, her Bible was on her chest, and she had a big smile on her face.

She left such an amazing legacy for me to follow.

Thank you, Granny.
Love, your Boy!

Boy, God brought you to me as my grandson. Some people say you are not mine by blood, and that is right, but you are mine by spirit, and that is much more important than of blood.

Boy, I am sorry for what has been done to you, but remember that

God did not do it to you, and what they have meant for bad, he will turn into good if you seek him first.

Boy, you are the true joy for me in my old age, and I am trying to tell you that your life is meant for greatness and you will inspire thousands of people with your story. You need to embrace it and then use every bad thing that has ever happened to you to glorify God.

Don't harbor hate, because it is a disease that has the power to wipe you out and everyone that you come in contact with on this earth.

I am an old woman that has learned from many mistakes. Please listen, because my words are running out and one day I will not be here to impart any more wisdom on you. At that time you need to become still and hear the words I taught you as a child.

I look forward to our visits each week. I have to tell you that every decision you make will either bring you closer to God or closer to serving the devil.

In your deepest pains of being sold as a child, they do not compare to the pain that God endured for you as he sent his son to die on the cross for your sins.

In your heartaches, you will either glorify the devil or you will use the pain to glorify God, and then use the pain to help other people.

I know it seems impossible that God could use you by being sold 751 times to help other people, but through your pain and heartache God will give you the key to unlock people's prison doors and help them heal. I do not know how, but I know God has shown me that my boy will lead a revival of healing heartaches one day. While on this earth I tried to love you as God has loved me, and I hope one day you will pass my love on to hundreds of thousands of people in the name of Jesus.

So my lovely boy, get quiet and hear the words of God and let him show you how to lead people out of their misery and into a loving life serving him. I will be watching from heaven to see how this will unfold for you.

To anyone that hears my lovely boy's words, know that he has been through the most horrible times to teach you how to move forward after a heartache. My boy has been given these words from God just for you, so apply what you learn and then pass them on to someone else in need. I need to know that my sweet boy has carried a burden that is so heavy that only God himself could heal him and give him this message of hope and love for you.

Please sit back with Granny and hear the words my lovely boy has been given to heal your mind, body, and spirit.

I love you Boy,
Granny

Chapter 1

David's Story

As with every new beginning, there comes a story—one which carefully defines the reason behind every new beginning. This particular tale is full of characters (one of which is you!) and without them (and you), the testimonies would be meaningless. Here is the One Spark Foundation story.

One Spark came to fruition with one man's journey in life. As with each and every one of us, our life could be described as an adventure novel. It is written by the characters we meet, the experiences we have, our highs and lows, our laughter, and our tears. Life is strange; you never know where you are going or how you are going to get there. Then, one day you look back to see you've been walking the entire time. You find yourself somewhere completely different than where you thought you were going or where you thought you would be.

At the One Spark Foundation, we'd like to think we are only beginning "Chapter One" of our voyage. The One Spark Foundation was created to change the world, one Spark at a time. We encourage others to perform willing acts of kindness each and every day. We call them Sparks!

We are a multi-program, non-profit 501(c)(3) organization, providing life-saving and life-enriching assistance through a total of thirteen programs:

1) S.T.O.P.: Stop Trafficking of People.
2) Trinity Farms: We grow food to help feed the needy and fund the One Spark Foundation.
3) Homeless Outreach: We feed five-star food to the homeless and needy. And, yes, we charge them to eat our food. The cost? A HUG!
4) Spark Programs: We go out and help random people with a Spark that they really need.
5) Wheels of Hope: We purchase a car for someone who is really in need.
6) Hospital Spark of Hope: We visit the hospital and give the kids bags of love filled with goodies.
7) Box of Love: We send boxes of love to our military people serving overseas, to people who are sick and need a Spark, and to children in the hospital.
8) Fire Truck of Hope: We have purchased a fire truck to give adults and children that are ill as well as people with disabilities a ride when needed. This is to provide them with hope to continue their fight.
9) School Spark Program: We travel all around the country talking to kids about the power of Kindness and the importance of making positive choices. This is a free service.
10) Covers for Conditions: We provide blankets for the homeless, sick kids, and even adults fighting a beast called cancer, heart disease, and mental illness. Other recipients include our troops returning from the war, suffering from lost limbs or PTSD. We hand out blankets to any and all that may need a kick in the pants from a Spark.
11) Helping Hands: We give clothing and furniture to people in need.
12) Santa's Workshop: We provide Christmas gifts for those who are in need, whether they are in hospitals or nursing homes. We also pay off layaways.

13) Free Hugs Campaign: We visit large venues and give out hugs. Many people at first try to refuse, and that is when we bring out one of our secret weapons—a small child—and they never refuse to give a hug.

We operate several different programs specifically designed to spread love and kindness, and encourage others to do the same. Spark Givers pride themselves in reaching out to others, both locally and around the world.

The beauty of the One Spark Foundation is that it is actually a very small part of changing the world. The One Spark Foundation has no paid employees, and what it accomplishes each day is with the help of volunteers. One Spark prides itself on having no monthly bills. Fortunately, the volunteers are able to work out of an office building that belongs to a Spark Giver. When each one of you performs Sparks where you live (combined with someone else's Sparks), a critical mass unfolds, creating an inferno of love that will never be extinguished. Spark Giving has to start at home. Only then can this practice exhibit positive, widespread effects for your town, your state, and, ultimately, the entire country.

To discover how we arrived at our present time, we need to follow the initial years of David's journey. Thus begins our narrative.

The founder of One Spark, David L. Hill, was motivated by his experiences from childhood to adulthood, as well as by the people he met along the way, to develop this foundation. The people he still meets every day become a part of another chapter in his story. Let's just say he is a custodian for a living. Giving you any more details about his day-to-day life now would be a distraction from the journey—which brings us to sharing his story.

I do have to say that many people remember David as the person he was in the past. I will be the first to admit that the old person was mean, nasty, filled with hate, prideful, and all about money and possessions.

To kick this off, I want to tell you about the difficulties David survived as a child. From the ages of four to eleven he was sold to men for fifteen dollars, 751 times. I realize that this is a difficult concept to grasp.

You might question how he knew he was sold exactly 751 times. David notched his bed each time it happened. The thing David still struggles with, and often says is this: "You think I would be worth at least twenty dollars." He deals a lot with his heartache and pain by using humor, so that other's hearts will not be burdened.

If being sold was not bad enough, the many men in David's mother's life (including several boyfriends and then a new husband), seemed to take pleasure in "straightening" David out. For them, this meant a good old-fashioned beating. David was the recipient of many of these as a young child.

At six years old, David was left alone for weeks while his mother shacked up with anyone she could find. Her idea of being "mother of the year" was remembering to leave boxes of Captain Crunch for David to eat while she went searching for her next conquest. Imagine being told on a daily basis that your mother wished she had aborted you because you were nothing but a heartache.

When David was seven, his two older half-brothers went to live with their mother. His half-sister and other half-brother moved in with their grandmother. David was left home alone, with a mother who didn't want him and a stepfather who hated him. He was extremely mean and rude to David and took it upon himself to hand out numerous beatings. Those whippings ended when David turned thirteen. He had grown bigger and taller by then and became quite capable of taking care of himself. One day, his stepfather entered his bedroom to administer the weekly thrashing, but it did not exactly turn out the way he anticipated. This caused an even bigger strain in David's relationship with his mom.

As David grew older, his mother told him she hated him because he looked just like his father, whom she despised with every fiber of her body. Try to picture going through life repeatedly trying to please two people—your mother and your father—but never once being able to satisfy either one of them.

David was dealt another blow when his mother came home one day before the summer of his junior year of high school and told him that she and her new husband were moving to Wichita. She added that he needed to find a place to live because there was no room for him where they were going, and she knew he wanted to graduate from the school he was in. He looked at her and said, "Okay." David dated a girl for a little while in high school, and her family took him in. Later, when David was hurt in a boating accident, his mother was notified, but she never went to visit him.

As David looks back on the sequence of events and the manner in which his mother and stepfather left, he's certain there were financial problems. Even so, it certainly would have been more favorable for his mother to have shown her child some love and compassion. He also reflects on his siblings and the countless pickles and anchors they've had to overcome as well over the years.

David went to Kingman High School, of which he has many fond memories. David hit it off with a guy named Vince who lived in his town. Without Vince and his family, David surely would have committed suicide.

One night Vince and David decided to drive their cars through a milo field and chase each other like they had seen in a movie. Those two boys were thick as thieves. Vince, being older, was always the one getting them into trouble—if you believe that, I am going to sell you some oceanfront property in Waterloo, Kansas. Imagine seeing two young men scouring a milo field to pick up the milo they had knocked down, because the farmer refused to file charges on them. Yes, this is the tiny town David lived in for his four years of high school.

David hung around the kids one year older than him, and there were a couple of them that stole his heart. Mike Paul had a soft spot for David, and Mike's mother treated him like he was her child. Mike and David have not really spoken since the day he graduated from high school. Mike played a huge part in David not throwing in the towel and committing suicide. David is forever grateful to Mike for saving his life.

The other person that made David feel loved on a daily basis was Sandra Dodge. She was his first crush and he was in love with her (even though he really had no clue what love was). The only problem was she was not in love with him. On the last day of school, Sandra told David that if the guy she was dating at the time did not work out, the two of them would get together. David was filled with joy! After she planted a big kiss on his cheek, he almost passed out.

David credits many people of Kingman High School for playing a huge part in him becoming the person he is today. Even though many bullies attempted (but were unsuccessful) to steal his joy, he refuses to name them—because he is better than that. David recalls standing up to one of the bullies and giving him a crack from a bat because he was such a jerk. At that time this guy was bigger than most of the students. However, David believes that today he is flying high with the eagles, and that jerk is still eating with the turkeys.

David was fortunate to have many people that liked him, but he really never felt like he had too many friends in high school. Luckily, there were always people that were nice to him. One of those kids, Justin Reed, spent quite a bit of time with him, and David ate many meals at his house. I know how thankful David is for Justin's friendship.

David was definitely blessed to have so many people be kind to him. However, I'm fairly sure that David was not very close to many people because of his guard being up—so he would not get hurt again.

From an early age, David remembers moving often and never having a chance to develop any friendships. When he finally entered high school, David rarely felt as though he belonged—except with one person—Steve. Steve was a talented singer who was full of love. Steve shared with David how he felt left out, just as David did. The two became best friends and developed an even closer relationship when they travelled to Europe to sing in the summer before their senior year. This was the first time David had travelled outside of the United States, and it was an amazing trip for him.

He and Steve sang with many other people in several venues across Europe and stayed with various families. Interestingly, one of those families had a room in their house where the cows lived. Waking up one morning, David recalls enjoying a delicious breakfast accompanied by warm cow's milk. Often, he and Steve talked and laughed into the wee hours of the morning. The next day they slept on the bus.

Steve was gifted with perfect pitch, and he was able to make anyone else (including David) singing with him sound really good. David and Steve were in their own world most of the time. Some of David's favorite memories of Steve include the times they went to the Rocky Horror Picture Show. They had a blast.

Many people picked on Steve, only because he was so different—but in a good way. Many thought of him as an easy target and, thus, took advantage of him. David often pleaded with them to leave Steve alone; some would, but others would not. Steven definitely did life his own way and never cared what anyone else thought of him. As David reflects upon Steve's life, he sees him as the most loving and brave person he ever met.

In Steve's senior year of high school he experienced an aneurism and was rushed to the hospital where he later passed away. This left David devastated. Even to this day, the wound is fresh and raw for him; he lost someone who knew him and loved him well—warts and all.

When Steve passed, David felt so crushed that he did not feel like going on with life. David was a person who always wore a big smile and acted as though nothing bothered him—inside he was a complete wreck.

David went on to college where he met a girl. She became pregnant and decided to have an abortion. Today, as David looks back, he is sure he would not have made a good father, at that point in his life. David wanted a child (but that would never happen), and it left him to think of the child who was aborted. David does not harbor resentment toward his college girlfriend, because as he says, "It would have been a mess for her to raise a child with me then."

David lived in fear of his father, who was a severe alcoholic. He often drank a gallon of vodka and several six packs of beer—nightly. Many times, after drinking his fill of alcohol, David's dad would lose himself to rage and turn into a man possessed with anger and a passion to dole out beatings.

I'm not sure whether David just wasn't smart enough or that he actually felt no fear. He would not back down from his father—no matter what. The first time his father gave him a severe beating, he cried. This, in turn, led his father to make fun of him. He taunted David by calling him names that can't be repeated here! David vowed from that point on that his father would never again have the satisfaction of seeing him cry.

Throughout all of the molestation and persistent beatings, there were always some caring people who gave hope that there could be a different life. There were very pivotal points in David's life when someone showed up to give him a Spark (Act of Kindness).

David's father was a man with many flaws. In addition to being an alcoholic, he was very hard hearted, prideful, arrogant, and obviously violent. Yet, despite all of his failings, his father possessed one redeeming quality. He was a giver, or as we call someone today—a Spark Giver. Once, when David was eight years old, his father told him to get in the truck because they were going to help someone. David was more than a little scared, as his father was very drunk at the time. That night they drove into town to a house David had never been to before. His father instructed him to get out of the truck, go to the front door, and knock. As any young child might, he knocked very softly, hoping no one would actually answer.

When his daddy got out of the truck and arrived at the door, his knock wasn't so gentle. He pounded on the door as if his life depended on it. After much hammering, a woman opened the door with a look of fear on her face. His father said he had heard she was having financial trouble and couldn't make her house payment. He pulled out seven, one hundred dollar bills and handed them to the woman. Then he gave her two coins and told her that no matter how bad things got, there would always be two people in her corner—he and his son. The woman began to cry and started to ask questions. However, David grabbed his father, thinking the worst was about to happen, and the two left—headed straight for the bar. By this point, yes, this eight-year-old boy was actually driving his father to the bar.

The saddest thing about this story is how David felt about his father and the situation. He was ashamed of his dad's alcoholism and the fear it had instilled in him and his siblings. Because of the circumstances, he never stopped to realize what a great and generous thing his father had done and continued to do. His father committed suicide in 1996. He had left David with seventy-five coins, which included half dollars, silver dollars, and other collector pieces.

David held onto all of these treasures for years, until one day it dawned on him what he was supposed to do with them. He knew he needed to give them away to people to give them hope and encouragement, just as his dad had done for others. He gave the coins to those he thought needed them at the time. Sadly, he regrets gifting some of these coins, as the recipients are no longer a part of his life. David now says, "I had to learn that when you give a gift, it is no longer yours. It does not matter if the person is still in your life or not. I pray for each person who has received a coin from me." David still has seventeen coins left. He's in the process of giving them to people he feels God wants him to give them to. It is possible that these acts inspire someone else to become a Spark Giver!

The next major Spark in David's life came from a teacher, Miss Penny Wood. She worked with him to ensure that he would indeed graduate from high school. She put in a lot of time and effort to give him the confidence he needed to succeed in life. She was a true "Spark Giver" to David. When it came time to enroll in college, he had no clue how to go about it. Miss Wood again took him under her wing and got the ball rolling. She proceeded to personally contact the high school board of education and, ultimately, received permission to enroll him in college.

David attended Emporia State University where he met the next Spark Giver—quite an integral part of his journey. Richard F. Reicherter was the Blue Key National Honor Society and Leadership Fraternity advisor at Emporia State. He offered David considerable wisdom regarding the business world and encouraged David to live by the "failure is not an option" approach.

What happened to change David? All of those previous chapters in his life!

You might be wondering who I am and how I know so much about David. That's an easy question to answer. I am his wife.

I will let David tell you in his own words. As David reflects upon his journey, here is what he says...

Once upon a time, I wasn't a very nice person. I was unhappy, prideful, insecure, selfish, and mostly an uncaring man who made a lot of people (mostly the ones who loved and cared for me) very unhappy. I never spent time with my family or cared what they were doing or what they thought. I didn't even take the time to answer their calls because I was a "big" man with an agenda, and it was all about me.

In 1996, while still in wretched misery I called "life," I met a waitress. She was just a "nobody" with an apron and a huge chip on her shoulder. That particular day, she had the good fortune of being the one waiting on me in the diner where she worked. I was in a bad mood, but it was evident that her disposition was even worse than mine. I can assure you that no niceties were exchanged between the two of us as she seated me at the far end of the diner, per my request. When she addressed me, my only responses to her contained irritability and complaints; she retorted with snapping and grumbling. We were quite the pair.

It was like two gladiators going to battle. After about thirty seconds of conversation with this waitress, I realized there were actually only one gladiator and a mouse; I happened to be the mouse.

After another thirty minutes of attempting to have a conversation with a woman who had more Ph.Ds. in "jerkology" than I did, I asked her if I could buy her a piece of pie and a cup of coffee. She told me what I could do with the pie and coffee. And, by the way, this didn't involving eating or drinking!

However, I'm a very persistent person and would not give up. Finally, after about an hour, I convinced her to sit down. She looked me in the eye and asked, "Crybaby, what seems to be your problem?" I told her I had just found my father who had committed suicide, and I felt like she should have been a little more compassionate. The truth is, I envisioned reaching over the table and choking her to death but refrained; I knew I did not look good in orange. Instead, I said, "Well, tell me what your problem is and why you are such a jerk."

She explained to me that she and her husband moved to this small town several months before he died of pancreatic cancer. He never told her he was sick and dying. She found herself in a place where she knew no one and considered the town as a whole to be about as friendly as an upset porcupine. Her two children and grandchildren came home for the funeral; this was all the family she had in the world. They stayed for about a week and then headed home. Halfway into their trip, a drunk driver went flying through the median, hit them head on, and killed all four people in the car. In a matter of one month, she had lost her entire immediate family.

At that point I thought, *Checkmate—she wins.*

I had arrived at the café around noon and did not leave until approximately 10 pm. During our conversation, I realized that things could be much worse for me than they actually were. I had such mixed emotions in my heart but knew that I needed to leave a note to let her know the profound impact she had on a young man's heart. My bill was $17.49, but I left one hundred dollars, a business card, and a note that read: "Thank you very much for your kind words; they turned a young man's heart from sadness and despair to a heart filled with gratitude for the time I had with my father."

I left and headed back to work. About two weeks later I received

11

a small box in the mail. I was (and still am) an avid watch collector, so I thought it was something I had ordered—until I shook the box. It sounded like a battery. I opened the box and immediately had to admit I was still acting like a jerk by not fully reading the note the waitress had sent me. I wanted to see the gift in the bottom of the box. Much to my surprise, I reached in and pulled out a .45 caliber bullet. I immediately thought, *You nut; I don't hunt with a .45*, recalling the point in our conversation where I told her I was an avid hunter.

As Paul Harvey says, "And now, the rest of the story...." I went back to the note and began to read where I left off. She wrote, "Little do you understand the Spark you gave an old woman's heart today. It changed my heart filled with grief and despair to knowing I have a mission left to do until I draw my last breath." Her mission was to Spark and spread kindness to every person who crossed her path. She went on to write, "I searched long and hard for a gift that would be worthy of the Spark you gave my heart, and the only thing I could come up with was the bullet I was going to use to commit suicide that night."

I have to admit I was not a very emotional person at that point in my life, but I found water leaking from my eyes that I later discovered were tears.

I never had another conversation with this waitress, but I promise you the footprint she left on my heart will be there until the day I die. I would love to tell you I started giving "Sparks" to others immediately, but I did not. It took over a year for this to sink in and for me to fully understand the mission God had given me. I will never stop Sparking and trying to make the world a better place for the next generation—until I draw my last breath.

As I poured my heart out to God about what he wanted me to do with this Spark stuff, a Bible passage kept coming to me. It was Matthew 22:34–40.

The GREATEST COMMANDMENT IN THE BIBLE, AND FOR PEOPLE LIKE ME, IT WAS THE BIBLE MADE EASY! Matthew 22:34–40 New International Version (NIV)

The Greatest Commandment

[34] Hearing that Jesus had silenced the Sadducees, the Pharisees got together. [35] One of them, an expert in the law, tested him with this question: [36] "Teacher, which is the greatest commandment in the Law?"

[37] Jesus replied: " 'Love the Lord your God with all your heart and with all your soul and with all your mind.'[a] [38] This is the first and greatest commandment. [39] And the second is like it: 'Love your neighbor as yourself.'[b] [40] All the Law and the Prophets hang on these two commandments."

I thought to myself, *I could do this—I could love God with all my heart, all my soul, and all my mind.* I was not sure in the beginning if I could love everyone else as I loved myself, but through time and practice, I started to get it down.

I want to point out just because I always try to do this, I fail often. This is why I say that I am the frog with the most warts. I do not pretend to have it all together, but I realize that I am a work in progress every day!

Since 1996, my passion for helping others has grown into a mission, and through this mission others have begun to catch the fire too. It is from this fire that the One Spark Foundation has grown. One Spark is simply defined as "doing something for someone other than yourself." This may include offering a kind word, opening or holding a door for someone, paying for someone's breakfast (my favorite!) or lunch, or letting a car in your lane during traffic. It doesn't have to cost a dime.

In my life I have had many pickles and anchors—sometimes because of stupid things I did. However, many of the pickles and anchors that transpired in my life I had no control over. I do not regret any of them happening to me because they have allowed me to develop a huge key ring (my stories) that I use to unlock other people's prison doors.

You may be wondering what all this talk of pickles, keys, and anchors is about. A pickle is a heartache that we have all had at some point in our lives. It could be a loss of a child, bankruptcy, loss of a business, a failed relationship, or a drug or alcohol addiction. Many other things can be regarded as pickles as well. An anchor is what shows up in your life when you do not deal with your pickle—that particular pickle festers until it becomes an anchor. Think of a boat anchor and what it is used for, and you will understand an anchor in your life. Once an anchor is dropped from a ship, it holds that vessel in place, not letting it move forward.

A key is a story of a pickle. This key holds the experiences you struggled with, but made it through, that you use to help others. I use my stories as keys when I put my key in someone's heart to unlock their prison door (their heartache that I have gone through). This helps them to heal faster and move forward with their life.

I do, however, regret all the pickles and anchors that I caused for many people in my life. I never learned to love myself, and that triggered a ripple effect in every relationship I had. I hurt many different people in many ways, and for that I am truly sorry. I can't change now what I have already done. I can only hope that the apology I am offering today will bring some closure to those I hurt.

I have lived a great life because I learned that, to really love people, one first must move from an internal thinker (all about me) to an external thinker (putting others first). When this happens, you will develop a new passion for life—one which you never knew might exist.

I have been blessed with the opportunity of sharing my keys (stories) with thousands of people. I am continually amazed at how this simple act has helped so many of these individuals to unlock their prison doors. In turn, they recognize their unique capacity and ability to positively move forward in life, while utilizing their stories (as keys) to help other people leave their prison—and never go back.

My prayer is that you take the time to examine your life to see if you have pickles or anchors that are keeping you from becoming the person you were meant to be. I also hope that you will recognize the importance of sharing your keys with other people so that these keys can help them heal and move forward in life.

If everyone would commit to doing one Spark a day, imagine how we could change the world!

"And remember, the best life we could ever live will be lived serving others."

One Spark can start a fire. The only unknown in this equation is—will it be your Spark that ignites an inferno that no person will ever be able to extinguish?

Many of us in our lives have had hard times when we did not know if we had exhausted God's grace. With everything that I had been through, and the way I handled what had happened to me, I was sure God was sitting on the throne with a cold compress on his head asking, "Why are you not listening to me?"

When I stood in front of a mirror, all I could see was shame, guilt, pain, loneliness, abandonment, and every shortcoming I had. I knew I was the frog with the most warts, and I decided that God would not want anything to do with damaged goods like me.

I was caught in the middle of my pickles and anchors, and I felt like my guilt and shame were stronger than God's grace and His love.

My life of abuse, neglect, and abandonment had caused me to put up a wall around me, so that no one could hurt me anymore. I had to build up such a wall to ensure both my safety and sanity. I often felt as though I lived inside of myself and that my life had no value. Every day I struggled with thoughts of suicide. Every time these thoughts started to win in my mind, I would get this overwhelming feeling that my life was worth something, and that I had a purpose. I bottled up all of my terrible experiences and, as a consequence, I chose to hurt others before they had a chance to hurt me. This was a very self-destructive behavior that led me straight into many fights.

I ventured out into the world with one mission in mind, and it had nothing to do with girls or alcohol. This was a mission to get into a fight. It was one of the only ways I knew how to deal with the hurt and pain of what had happened to me.

I moved through life getting people before they could get me. If that meant lying, cheating, stealing, manipulating, or even using force to get what I wanted, that is what I would do. I did all these bad things in the name of my painful childhood experiences, not caring that the people I was hurting had nothing to do with what had happened to me as a child. I felt as though I had a "go jump in the lake" card, and I would use it without any remorse.

I had so much hate inside of me that the only way I thought I could get it out was to hurt people mentally or physically, and that is what I did. I was arrested many times for fighting, but got away with it many more times than I got caught. It did not matter where I was: at a wedding, church, family function, or even a bar. If you pushed my button, I promise you that a fight would break out.

As I look back on the tons of fights I got into, I have to say that they happened because of me not dealing with my past hurt and letting others occupy mind space they were not paying rent on. Plus, there's the fact that I had no personal relationship with God.

How do I forgive someone that did not deserve to be forgiven?

I know that as a Christian, it is imperative to forgive others, or we will not be forgiven by our Heavenly Father. I would sit and ask myself how in the world I could forgive someone that sold me 751 times. How do I forgive someone who was abusive, mean, and downright cruel?

I had to deal with the fact that the people I loved and trusted hurt me and showed no remorse, while acting as though they had done nothing wrong.

Every one of us has struggled with a pickle or an anchor at some point in our lives, and many of the things that happened to us were not our faults; these events make many people cringe when they hear our stories.

Numerous times I asked myself, in the midst of my many battles and thoughts of suicide, *Why should I forgive someone that did me so wrong and caused me so much pain and heartache?* I knew why, based on what the Bible said, but I needed more than a God that I could not see or hear to direct my reasoning—or so I thought.

This is when I woke up one day from a nap and remembered my dream. In that dream I could see myself smashing my pickles and anchors into keys. I could remember my Granny telling me that one day I would use my keys to help heal people.

Some of you might be thinking right now, *I never went through anything like you did, so my failed marriage, failed business, bankruptcy, loss of a loved one, and many other circumstances that might have happened to me are not as bad as what you went through.* STOP thinking like that because what you are going through right now is just as bad for you as what I went through. Do not put degrees on bad, because bad is bad and it all sucks.

I knew my dream was from God, and I started to realize that the only way I was ever going to get free from the heartache, pain, guilt, and the feeling that the only way I would ever get better, was to take my life, just like my father did. I knew that from this day forward, I would see my pickles and anchors as keys. My keys are my stories of all the bad things that happened to me. I knew that the only way that I was ever going to heal was to put my key (my story) into the heart of someone that was going through what I had gone through to unlock their prison door that had held them in a place where they could now move forward. I would share what I had gone through, and then I would share how I moved forward. This, in turn, would speed up their healing and help them develop their own keys, so they could help others.

My desire for this book is to help people realize that bad things happen to all of us, some of no fault of our own and some because of poor choices. It does not matter why they happened. The only thing that really matters is that you understand that you have the power to turn your pickles and anchors into keys.

I want to address something right up front. I am a Christian, but that does not mean you have to be a Christian for this to work. I want you to know that God did help me, but I know that if you have no faith, you can still turn your pickles and anchors into keys. You need to realize that there are many people whom your keys can help—the only unknown is whether you will use them.

A chapter recently closed in my life. I was never very close to my mother. The reasons don't really matter at this point in life. However, what does matter is that we were able to spend time together in her final days. We both were made whole in our relationship, and both of us got what we needed before she died. We reconciled our relationship through the power of Jesus Christ!

On the day before my mother died I asked her if she had asked Jesus for forgiveness, and she said (only as my mother could have), "David, I am not that stupid. Yes, I asked to be forgiven, and now I am asking why he has left me here so long."

I told my mother that day that her earth mission had not been completed yet—that's why she was still alive and present. She touched so many people while in the hospital as well as in the care home.

Through this journey of healing and speaking to so many people, I have found a commonality in their responses to my particular story. They say something like, "Well, David, I did not have it *that* bad." In reality, it was the worst thing that they could have had to deal with. Pain to each person is real. No one should ever be made to feel that their heartache is "less than" someone else's—because to the person dealing with it, it was horrible.

I have figured out that the best life I am ever going to live will be lived serving other people.

Love, David A2J

Chapter 2

Miss Bunny

My name is Miss Bunny. No, that's not my real name, but let's just say it is for now. I was asked to write my story and tell you how I overcame my pickles and anchors.

I was a very rebellious child and really did not have much chance to become anything other than what I became. You see, my mother was in the (business) of sex, and the only thing she cared about was the money she made.

I was the youngest of four girls, and we all were introduced into the business at the ripe old age of thirteen. Yep—thirteen—because men loved to be with a young girl who had never been with anyone else before. These guys brought in the big bucks. So on my thirteenth birthday, I had sex with a man who was fifty-seven. He was mean, and the things my mother let him do to me were horrible.

As I look back on my life, I can now see that my mother was solely breeding to have girls, to pimp them out, to make money. My oldest sister followed in my mother's footprints, and she started to recruit innocent troubled girls who needed money in order to live. At one time, there were over twenty young girls working for my mother and sister. The next two oldest girls in my family hated my mother and my sister, and what was worse is that they hated themselves.

I can remember that my mother would buy me nice things. I thought it was because she loved me, but I later figured out that it was because she wanted men to pay more for me. I can remember many days where I had sex with ten married men. Many of them would tell me that the only reason they were coming to me was because their wives would not do what I was willing to do. I wanted to tell them that I was not willing, only afraid of what my crazy mother would have her boyfriend do to me.

At the age of nineteen, I became pregnant, and my mother did not seem to mind. This made me nervous. It did not take me long to figure out why she was not mad. She wanted me to get pregnant, hoping it would be a girl.

I did find out that I was having a girl, and that is when I decided that I was leaving and had to take care of myself. My mother would use mind tricks to keep me and my sisters from running away. She would say to each one of us, "If you leave, I'll make your sisters suffer." For the longest time I bought into this reasoning and stayed home. However, when I found out I was pregnant, I knew I had to leave.

I waited until my mother and her boyfriend got so drunk that they passed out. I went into their room, took all the money I could find, and left. I got on a bus, headed for a place where I knew no one, and no one knew me.

I arrived in this town where I met a man who told me that he could help me get back on my feet. I thought, *I know what that means.* I asked him what he wanted to do to help me. He then relayed to me his story of being sold hundreds of times by his mother to men for money. He told me how he changed his pickles and anchors into keys so that the keys could unlock other people's prison doors.

I started to think about what he was saying to me. I fought it, until one day he told me that my hands were so bound up with hate, that they could not catch a blessing from God. He said to me, "If you don't let go of all that hate inside, it will destroy you." He told me that my hate had me anchored down to my situation. He added, "Unless you forgive the people in your past, you will never have a future."

One day, I decided to look for my mother and sisters on the web pages they used to advertise on, and I found my older sister. I sent her a message and asked how everyone was doing. She replied, "Mom is in a care home, and our sisters are still working hard."

I wrote my mother a letter and told her I forgave her for what she did to me; I told my oldest sister the same thing. I never thought that I would hear back from either one of them, but I did. My mother made excuses for her actions, and my oldest sister told me that I was missing the good life.

My mother passed away at the age of forty-eight, my oldest sister was arrested for selling girls, and our two sisters committed suicide. I felt as though I failed them. In reality, though, I was not able to help them until I helped myself.

It is amazing to see how one man's story has touched so many people. Yes, the man I met was David. I'm a college graduate, married, and enjoy working with people who have pickles and anchors they need to change into keys.

Yes, I made it out. I have a wonderful husband and five great kids. I strive to help as many people as I can change their pickles and anchors into keys.

Many people tell me that their pickles and anchors are not as bad as mine. This is when I relay to them what my Yoda master told me, "Your pickles and anchors are yours, and they are bad to you. You see, everyone has a pickle, and a lot of people have anchors. We don't want to compare them, because to each person, their pickles and anchors are the worst things—to them."

Here is what I hope you get out of this book. We all have pickles, and many of us have anchors. The sad thing is that many of us have never dealt with them and then converted them into keys. Remember—your keys have the power to open prison doors that may remain locked, unless your key is interred into their hearts. These concepts helped to change my life, and I hope you will benefit from them as well.

Love, Blessed—even after all the pickles and anchors.
P.S. It will not be easy, but it will be worth it.

Chapter 3

David's Sayings

1. A friend is someone who knows your past, helps you build your future, and loves you just the way you are.
2. We have the right to get angry with people, but we do not have the right to get ugly with them. The words we speak today will be planted in the hearts of those who receive them forever! We need to choose our words wisely—for if we do not, they may haunt us or someone else forever!
3. Success will not be measured in dollars and cents but by how we love all the people we come in contact with in life.
4. When we seek revenge against our enemies, we find that we are no better than them. It is only when we forgive them that we become superior to them.
5. Failure is knowing that you have the ability to help someone but choose not to.
6. We must leave people in a better place than where we found them.
7. True friendship is unconditional. It does not come with demands, but with understanding.
8. Our success will not be measured by our status or the amount of money we have gained. It will be measured by how we treated the people who we came in contact with.

9. The mark of a great person is how they treat the people who have nothing to offer them (no favoritism).
10. Life is full of tests. Unfortunately, life never gives out the answers before the tests.
11. A foolish man thinks that happiness can be found in things, and a wise man knows that it can only be found in the heart.
12. A man who dies rich but never had a true friend…was never rich at all.
13. The true test of our character is what we do when no one is around and there is no chance of getting caught.
14. It is often said that money and success are the root of all kinds of evil. The truth is that they only amplify what is in a person's heart.
15. Friendship cannot be bought or sold but is worth more than all the money in the world.
16. Happiness does not and will not happen by chance. IT IS A CHOICE!
17. Excuses are the thieves that will rob our lives of any chance of success.
18. Life can never defeat us until we quit.
19. Procrastination is like going to an 80 percent off sale the day after the sale began. All that is left is the junk that no one else wanted.
20. If we are ever going to find the pot at the end of the rainbow, then there will be times that we have to deal with the rain.
21. We may not be able to lift the load off of our friend's back, but we surely can lighten the load.
22. Love does not come with conditions, but with Grace.
23. The greatest revenge you can ever give to an enemy is forgiveness. Nothing will upset them more.
24. The most essential factors of success are persistence and the knowledge that failure will never be an option.
25. It is much easier to oppose something than it is to get involved.

26. If we enter the game without the determination to win, then we have already lost.

27. The greatest conflict that we will ever face will not be with another person but with ourselves.

28. There are many failures in life, but the greatest failure we can experience is the failure to start.

29. It seems as though no one is paying attention until you make a mistake.

30. The best life we can live is a life spent serving others.

31. There are far better things to do with our time than GOSSIP.

32. We all have something to offer the world. The only question is—will we?

33. In order for us to perfect the art of leadership, we must first perfect the art of serving.

34. Love is not an emotion but a will, and sometimes we must will ourselves really hard to love that special person! In the end it is worth it!

35. If we choose not to make a plan for our lives, life may give us a plan that we do not like (Lord willing).

36. Here is to a new day and another chance for all of us to get it right.

37. True friends will be there to cheer us on and help us up when we are down.

38. A compliment is one of the greatest gifts that we can give because of its ability to warm the heart.

39. We need to live our lives each day with the three Es: Energy, Enthusiasm, and Empathy.

40. We can succeed at almost anything as long as our belief never waivers, and we never quit.

41. Respect is treating people the way we would want to be treated even though we might not feel like they deserve it.

42. Character is taking responsibility for the things that we mess up and not trying to pass the blame.

43. A loving heart has the power to change the world.

44. Being kind to people is a habit! Unfortunately, so is being mean.

45. When we rise in the morning we need to tell ourselves that the cutoff for being unhappy was three hours ago.

46. If we fail to forgive, we become slaves to bitterness.

47. If you are looking for a test to determine if your mission on earth is complete, here it is—if you are alive, it is not complete. The best life lived is one serving others.

Chapter 4

Individual Stories

I have been blessed to be the Head Custodian of the One Spark Foundation, and I say that with the most sincere heart. I do not believe that I am any more important to the One Spark Foundation than the people who have written and shared their Spark stories.

As you know, I am a Christian, and because of that I do not believe that anything in life is random. If you have taken the time to read the beginning story of the One Spark Foundation, you know why we call our acts of kindness—Sparks.

The stories that you are about to read have been sent to us by everyday people like you and me. However, what makes them so special is the fact that they (in their own Spark story) have become experts in the art of being Master Spark Givers.

They could have reacted in many different ways to their situations, but they chose love and kindness to be their anthem.

I hope that before you begin to read these amazing Sparks, you get yourself a box of tissues and then be prepared to have your heart lifted, broken, and overwhelmed with joy.

Love, David A2J

NEVER TOO OLD

Psalm 92:12–14 New International Version (NIV)
[12] The righteous will flourish like a palm tree,
    they will grow like a cedar of Lebanon;
[13] planted in the house of the LORD,
    they will flourish in the courts of our God.
[14] They will still bear fruit in old age,
    they will stay fresh and green,

Becky, a seventy-nine-year-old woman, shared the following story with One Spark.

I was given an awesome Spark by both your organization and a few high school girls a few years back. You painted my house, fixed my roof, and put some landscaping in. I have been sitting back on my bottom for two years and have done nothing. I used these excuses: I am too old; I don't have enough money; and so on. So one day I got up and said, "Today is the day I pay it forward." I started to bake some goodies and knew right where they were going to end up. I baked twelve dozen cookies and then called my friend to come pick me up and take me to the old peoples' homes. I gave them all out, and they were so happy. Soon I found more places to take these little goodies that seemed to put smiles on everyone's faces. We took them to hospitals, schools, police stations, fire stations, and many other places.

I got sick and was worried that my goodies would not get baked. I called my daughter, who lives far away, and asked her to come home to help me. She must have thought I was going to die because she rushed right home. I asked her if she would grant a dying woman her last request. I knew I was not dying because I only had a gallstone. She said yes, and I told her that I needed her to call some women from the church and help me bake for my friends. She said, "Mom, that's no problem at all!"

Well, it didn't take her long to call me back again and say she did not feel she could pack eighty-five dozen cookies. She is a doctor, you see, and simply offered to purchase them herself. I said, "No, I'll do it." She said it would get done. She called the church, and the church got lots of women and sent them over. Well, now problem number two was that I had a kitchen only big enough to fit me and one dog. So the women split the baking duties, and everyone went to their homes to bake.

My precious doctor had an idea. She called a boy she went to school with, and he immediately came over. She told him to redo my kitchen and make it fit for a queen. I came home four days later and found One Spark and many of my friends in my home. I must say that they added 600 square feet to my kitchen. The kitchen is not the point, but what is the point is that we all need to get off of our bottoms and give back to the world and make it a better place.

I love what One Spark has done for me and my little world. I am almost seventy-nine years old, and if I can do it, then all of you should be able to do something. Don't be like me and waste several years and not get to see kindness in action. As my friend would say, "The best life we can live will be a life serving others. Failure is when we have the ability to help someone and we choose not to. Don't get hung up on what you can't do. Get hung up on what you can do!"

Lots of love, Becky.

THE CHAMP

"This is how we know what love is: Jesus Christ laid down his life for us. And we ought to lay down our lives for our brothers and sisters." 1 John 3:16 (NIV)

This is my story of joy and heartbreak. I have four children and have tried to do the best that I could do in raising them. My youngest child was a boy who had a lot of promise to go far in life. He was a great athlete and a good student. He won state in wrestling three years in a row and had offers to wrestle anywhere he wanted. He was a great running back and still holds records, but this great and shining star dimmed one night with a choice he made to try a drug that everyone said would not be any big deal. "Just take a little hit of this crack and it will make you feel alive."

This is the day that his life changed and would never be the same. We immediately noticed that something was not right with him. He became angry and seemed to be very sad. He went downhill very fast, and within five months he had lost all chances he had to go to college. For the next few years he lived on the streets with the main purpose of getting high. He would do absolutely anything to get high, no matter what that meant. He had been in and out of jail over the next few years. He would go to eat in a little park in Wichita, Kansas. He would call and tell me about this crazy guy who charged him and others to eat. At first I got so mad—until he told me that this guy charged them a hug.

My son was drawn to this man who always told him that he loved him. My son said he would go back several times to eat and he would have to give the man another hug. The man always said things like, "If you go back to Burger King for seconds, would it cost you more money?" and "Don't try to steal from me...GIVE ME MY HUG!" He told my son that he could do whatever he wanted to do and that he needed to be the man he was meant to be. He told him that he was put on this earth for a reason.

My son was clean for a year and a half and then moved home. He called his park friend every day to tell him how he was doing. My son visited all the nearby schools to speak about making good choices. He loved giving back and wanted to make sure that no child had to go through what he went through because of poor choices. He was working for our family business, and he was our best employee.

We live in a place where the winters can be brutal, and even deadly, if you don't use your head. My son heard that there was a lady and two kids who had slid off the road and needed help. My son jumped into his big truck and went out to help them. He found them

ours, finally removed their car from the ditch
n safely. He came to our house and said he
hey were now safe in town. He said his hands
im. We said to him, "Son, you really need to
om." He replied, "Oh, I'll be fine after I take a
ke a shower, and my husband and I lost track of
iter, I went to check on my son and found him
id a massive heart attack and was already gone.
gh his belongings, I found a note in his wallet
David, the man in the park. It read, "You are
n as a loser. The past will not determine your
legacy. If you want a great legacy, make it from this day forward. I
love you buddy, and in my eyes you are a champ."

There were over 1,500 people at his funeral, and most were kids
who wanted to tell us what my son had done for them. He left an
incredibly memorable legacy for the time he was clean. The greatest
thing he did was give me a year and a half back to be with my son.
We did everything together in those last days. I am not sad, because
I know I will see him again one day.

The Champ's mom.

Woman Mean as a Rattlesnake

*"People can tame all kinds of animals, birds, reptiles, and fish, but no
one can tame the tongue. It is a restless evil, full of deadly poison." James
3:7–8 (NLT)*

*"For you are all children of God through faith in Jesus Christ."
Galatians 3:26 (NLT)*

I am a single mother who has left a very abusive relationship after
ten years. That is not the story I want to tell you about. I have five
children and they are the loves of my life. They range in ages from
four to seventeen. We have been struggling a lot financially because

their father will not pay child support. For some time now I have been in a poor, poor-me state of mind. My daughter came home one day from school and said to me, "Mom, my life has been changed today!" When I asked her how, she lit up like a Christmas tree and told me about a guest speaker who came to her school. She told me all about the One Spark Foundation and their mission to change the world, one Spark at a time.

She asked me if we could start doing Sparks for other people and I said, "No, because no one has ever been there to help us." She smiled and said, "Okay." She then told me that I was her favorite mother in the whole world. About a week later, I was called into the living room for a family meeting. They had the little one start the meeting by saying, "We need to be nice because the baby Jesus wants us to be." Then, one by one, each of my children got up and told why they wanted to do Sparks for other people.

The last to speak was my oldest daughter, and as I sat and listened to her, I felt as though I was in court listening to a brilliant lawyer. When she finished, she asked if I was with them or against them. I told them I was in. We started doing little things for people, like baking a pie or cleaning up their yards. We also started our own One Spark pit crew. We practiced changing tires in our driveway. Then we would go out and help people on the streets. We asked a local printer if he would donate cards for us, and he did.

Then, one day, we found out that a lady (who owned most of the town we lived in) had broken her hip, and no one would help her because she was so nasty. We decided that we would go and take her a few things and ask if we could help out any other way. We started helping her, and it seemed as though no one wanted to stay for very long because she was meaner than a rattlesnake. I found out that I would be losing my job at the end of the month, and I was very scared about what we were going to do.

We went to visit Miss Nasty (Helen) on Monday, and my little one told her son that I was losing my job. He approached me about working for his mom full time. I told him that I did not know if I could handle her nasty attitude. He told me that his mother looked forward to our family visits. He asked me, "How much money do you need in order to accept this job?" I told him what I was making at my current job and he said he would not be able to pay me that amount. I started to say something when he offered another wage. The amount was 2.5 times more than I was making. I asked him why he would pay that much and he told me that is what they were paying the service that sent out the other people. I started to cry and said to him, "It will not matter how nasty she gets, I will do my job until she is well."

I have been working with Helen for five months now, and I've had to read the One Spark site a lot. I have really been down on myself for getting nasty with her a few times. But, then I continue to read Dave's posts about the times he has failed, and that gives me the strength to keep on keeping on. One day, my whole family was at Miss Nasty's house, and my little one went into her room to work her up. She was mad and started to yell, and that is when the most amazing thing happened. Her son and I met in the hallway outside her door when we heard my daughter telling Miss Nasty what she thought of her attitude. We heard her say to Helen, "You are so mean! You need to have your mouth washed out with soap, a spanking, and to be put in time out!" She went on to tell Helen how she had hurt her feelings. "You are just not very nice, and I don't want to play with you anymore."

What we heard next shocked her son and me so much that we stood there for over three minutes while the two of them spoke. Helen said to my daughter, "I'm so sorry I hurt you, honey. I do not want to stop playing with you!" My daughter insisted that if she and Helen were to continue playing together, then she would have to tell everyone she was sorry.

The very next day Helen invited me into her room and asked if I would call her son and ask him to pick up my children after school and bring them to the house. When they arrived, she called each of us into her room, one by one, and said she was sorry for how she treated us. Her son was the last visitor, and he was in there for over an hour. When he came out, I could tell he had been crying, and I asked if he was all right. He said, "I've never been better! My mother just apologized for the way she has treated me all these years."

Helen got better, and on the way to her last doctor visit I told her that it had been great working for her. I added that I was going to miss her. She looked at me funny and asked if I had gotten a better job and I said no. She said, "That's good, because I still need you and your family." She told me that I needed to think about moving my family into her home because she was going to need a lot more help. Yes, she has a big house.

Love, a grateful Spark giving family.

P.S. Dave, we know that what you do is hard, but if you had not been there for us, our family would have been lost. We are not the one person you were looking for, we are the six people. You changed six people's lives forever. So when life gets you down, pick up this letter and know you have changed six lives. You must never stop what you are doing, because the world needs you and One Spark.

DRUNK, NOT SUGAR COATED

Galatians 5:21 New International Version (NIV)

[21] and envy; drunkenness, orgies, and the like. I warn you, as I did before, that those who live like this will not inherit the kingdom of God.

I'm a father of four great kids, and I have been married for over fifteen years. In those fifteen years I have been an alcoholic for most of them. There are usually two types of drunks in the world of alcoholics: the nice ones and the mean ones. I hate to admit it—and Dave says that he was not a nice person—but I can tell you that I have held fifty Ph.Ds. in mean and nasty. My wife would always be on me about what my drinking was doing to our kids and to me. I told her that I would quit when I got ready to quit.

I would get drunk every night but was able to function well

at work. I did my job so well that no one knew what was going on at home. I never went to parties or functions because I knew that someone would find out that I had a problem.

Then a lady at work introduced me to One Spark by telling me how the organization had helped her son and their family. I started to read all the great things that they were doing and after about six months of reading, I sent David an email telling him about how bad my life was and why I had become a drunk. He emailed me back asking for my phone number and a good time for him to call. I sent him an email back and could not wait for the King Pin of Spark giving to call me and tell me how he was sorry for the rotten life that I had. The phone rang and I was surprised when Dave asked me if I wanted him to sugar coat what he had to say. I thought that I would not tell my wife and kids the bad things Dave was going to say, so I told him to give it to me straight. After about five minutes, I wished I had asked him to sugar coat it. I thought, *Who does this man think he is? He knows nothing about the world of an alcoholic.* Then Dave told me his story about both of his parents being drunks and the damage it did to him as a young boy. I started to complain, and that is when Dave finally said, "Are you a man or a mouse?" He told me to shut my mouth and realize that there were people who wanted to love me and be around me. He continued with, "You also need to make a choice to quit drinking or move out of the house, because the damage you are doing to your children is terrible and will last forever." Dave asked me if I was an honest man, and I told him that I was a drunk, not a liar. He said, "Make me a promise," and I said, "Okay."

When I got home that night I sat down with my family and we talked for over three hours. I found out there was a lot of hurt and anger in my house. I cried more than I've ever cried in my life. That day I made a promise to them that I would never drink again. And, as of today, it has been seventy-five days since my last drink.

One Spark has saved my family, and I know Dave doesn't like this, but he is now and will always be my hero. One last thing I want to say about Dave is that he is my hero because he never judged me and the love of my Lord Jesus Christ. He told me all of his faults first, and it made it much easier knowing that we all have problems.

Love, Mr. Sober.

SPARK AND OLD MAN

"So anyone who becomes humble as this little child is the greatest in the Kingdom of Heaven." Matthew 18:4 (NLT)

I am a seventy-seven-year-old man and I would like to share a story. My granddaughter told me all about One Spark and what they had done at her school. I love it when my granddaughter prints off the Sparks that are being done and brings them to me to read. You see, I lost my wife a few years ago and have not felt very happy since.

One day my granddaughter came in and said, "Grandpa, I made you and me our own Sparks book so we can log all the Sparks that we do." I smiled and we went out the door, and we were on the hunt for who we could help. We saw a lady on the side of the road, so we pulled in behind her to see what was wrong. She told us that she had run out of gas. I had a five-gallon gas can that I keep at the farm, so we left to get the can and then put gas in her car. We followed that by giving her a One Spark card.

My granddaughter and I had done several Sparks together, but I had never done one by myself. Let me tell you about my first one.

My neighbor's husband ran off with another woman, leaving my neighbor and her three kids without any money. I saw the electric company lady walking up to my neighbor's house with something in her hand. I asked what she was doing, and she said she was putting a shut-off notice on the door. She wasn't very nice. So I asked her if she wanted to make a couple of people happy today, and she replied, "It depends." I told her that I wanted to pay the bill and the lady asked, "What? Do you know how much it is?" I told her I was sure I wanted to pay it and I asked her how much it was. The total was $467.91.

I told her that sounded like a small price to pay to make someone happy. The lady asked why and I told her that I wished she had a computer to get onto the internet. She got into her car and pulled out a laptop that she could get on the internet with.

I had her pull up the One Spark website and read the beginning story of One Spark. She started to cry and said, "This is awesome." I asked her if she would help me pay the bill, and she said she could call the office and pay the bill. She did and I gave her my credit card and the bill was paid. Then I asked her to write on the shut-off notice that her One Spark angel had paid the bill, and the only thing the angel asked for was that she pass it on. The electric lady and I hugged and cried a little bit. She asked me for a few cards and I gave them to her. This is the greatest thing I have done in my life. My only regret is that my wife isn't here to share the experiences.

LIFE BACK – WIFE OF FIFTY-FIVE YEARS DIED – MAN FINDS NEW LIFE

"A wife of noble character who can find? She is worth far more than rubies." Proverbs 31:10 (NIV)

I have to tell you a little about me for this story to make sense. My wife and I got married when I was sixteen and she was only fifteen. No, she was not pregnant. I knew I had found the best woman in the world; she liked me and said she wanted to marry me. I thought she was blind and dumb, so I knew we needed to get married before she changed her mind.

We were married for fifty-five years and those were the best fifty-five years of my life. We never had children because she was unable, but I didn't care because I had married the best girl in the world. She would help anyone that needed help. My wife would have loved you, David, and you two would have been best of friends.

Many people said she was doing these nice things to show off. No sir! She did them for the love of Jesus. After my wife died, I gave up, became mean, and hated God so much. This all changed one cold night, and I mean it was really cold, with freezing rain and wind blowing like a jet engine. I was out in that crazy weather because I had to go to the store to make sure that I had enough supplies if I got snowed in. My car started to slide and I slammed into a curb, knowing that I needed to get out to check the damage. Then this funny looking fire truck pulled in behind me. It was not a fire truck. It was the One Spark wagon! This man asked, "Sir, would it be all right if I changed your tire for you?" I asked how much and he said, "Free." I thought, *I'm not as dumb as you*. He handed me a card and said he had to run to help someone else.

I had this card for a year before I did anything. The lady who lives next to me has three kids and their dad is a deadbeat. I had been pretty mean to her since my wife passed away. So I talked to her and asked what she was going to do for the kids for Christmas, and she said, "Nothing, because we have no money." It was her day off, and I said that I needed her help. She asked, "Doing what?" I replied, "Shopping for your kids." That day we spent nine hours shopping and spent over $7,000. It was the most fun I have had since my wife died.

Later I told the young lady that there was something that I wanted to give her. I took her into my house and told her, "My wife loved jewelry; every one of her pieces are in this box. I want you to have the jewelry with one condition—never sell it."

She asked me why I was doing this and if I was dying. To that I replied, "No, I am living again."

David, I know it was you in that truck because I saw you on TV feeding the homeless. Never stop what you are doing; I have my life back because of you and One Spark.

SUNSHINE – BOY SINGS TO HIS DYING NEWBORN SISTER

"A friend loves at all times, and a brother is born for a time of adversity." Proverbs 17:17 (NIV)

I heard a story of a little boy. When he found out his mother was pregnant with his little sister, he was happy and started to sing, "You Are My Sunshine." Every day, several times a day, he would run over to his mom and sing to his little sister. He did this day after day, week after week, and month after month.

One day his mom told him that they needed to go to the hospital because his sister was coming and they wanted to see her. Once at the hospital, there were some complications, and the doctor told the family that the little baby girl would probably not make it through the night. The boy wanted to see his sister, but the hospital would not allow kids into the ICU, so his mom decided to sneak him in. She knew it might be his only chance to see his sister alive. He followed his mother into the room, and at first he was a bit scared because he saw all of the tubes that were attached to his sister.

The head nurse came around the corner and said to the mom in a hateful tone that kids were not allowed. Without the mom telling him to, her son started singing to his sister. The nurse noticed that the little girl's heart rate started to slow and she told the little boy to keep singing. He kept singing "You Are My Sunshine" for over ten minutes. The nurse noticed that the baby's color had gotten better and her vitals were perfect.

You see, we all have the power in our words to breathe life into another or suck life out. Today, I hope you choose life!

Fifty-Nine-Year-Old Jerk – Not Sure if Anchor to Key?

"Those who are kind benefit themselves, but the cruel bring ruin on themselves." Proverbs 11:17 (NIV)

This is a note to Dave, the founder of One Spark.

Hi Dave. I have to first say that you could never have been the biggest jerk in the world, because that has been my title for over two years now. I took over a family business and never cared about anything but results. If you did not perform, you did not stay. We did continue to grow, despite my nasty nature. I would burn through people so fast it seemed as though there was a revolving door in our building. Sometimes I would do little things just to make people mad.

I was in Kansas for a meeting with a company we support and got a flat tire. You stopped and changed it. I was not very nice to you, and I will never forget what you said to me. "Sir, I am a recovering jerk, and I am liable to relapse at any time." You looked at me with that big smile and said, "You all done?" I reached into my wallet and pulled out fifty dollars to pay you, and again you gave me that big Kansas smile. You reached into your pocket and gave me a One Spark Card. I asked what it was, and again with a smile you asked if I could read. I told you yes and then you said, "Read the back of the card." I did and asked, "What is the catch?" Again, you smiled and said, "Nothing, just being kind." You went on to tell me to pass it on because my kindness just might save someone's life. The next thing I knew I was getting a big bear hug from you, and you said to me, "Thanks for letting me serve you."

I carried this card around with me for five years before I did anything for anyone. The one good thing I did do was to read all of your stories and acts of love from your website and Facebook site. I found myself sitting in my office with the door locked because I cried after reading each story. Finally, I introduced the One Spark program to my company. When I did, I think they thought I was dying, or at least wished I was.

I need to back up a bit. I have to start with my wife of thirty-seven years. She lost her wedding ring nine years earlier and I told her I would not get her a new one. Well, I bought her a four-carat ring, went home, told her I loved her, and gave her the ring. She asked me if I was having an affair. I said no and told her about you. She did not believe me, so I got on your website and called the number to talk to you.

My wife started to talk to you and she repeated what I told her about how we met. She asked if you remembered me and you said, "Yes, because I never forget a self-proclaimed jerk." My wife laughed and said, "You do know him." You guys spoke for over an hour and you asked her to go to Facebook or your website and read the beginning story. She did and so did I. We both began to cry. At that moment we vowed to make a difference in the world for the rest of our lives. I called my office in the morning and told them that I wanted everyone to gather in the office at 10 AM.

My wife and I went to the bank and got out enough money to give each person $500 cash. Afterward, my wife said, "I didn't believe you'd really do that, but after all, you did give me a ring!" I did do it and have not looked back.

I'm doing ten Sparks a day, like you, Dave. You are my hero, and you changed my life at work and at home. We have two sons and a daughter. Not one of them at that time worked with us in our family business. Now they all do and they love it! I would never have made these changes if it wasn't for One Spark. So, if a fifty-nine-year-old man can change, anyone can!

I made my donation (my daughter did) on your Pay Pal account and will do so every month. I hope that more people will give a dollar, two, or maybe ten dollars a month. Imagine what you could do if you had more funds! I love you, brother, My Spark Giver.

LIFE SAVED – MOM WANTED TO KILL HERSELF

"Be completely humble and gentle; be patient, bearing with one another in love." Ephesians 4:2 (NIV)

Dear Dave, I wanted to write this letter to let everyone know what you have done for me and my family. I am a mother of four children and have suffered from depression for over ten years now. I have attempted suicide several times and the doctors have tried everything they know to help me, yet it always seemed to end up the same way.

Then my daughter came home one day and told me that they were having a program at her school to help with bullying and learning to be kind. She said, "The principal told us that the parents could also come if they want to." I said, "There's no way I can go to that; I have too much stuff to do!" This was code for 'I did not want to go out in public.' I am not sure how my family has put up with me through these dark days, but they have.

My daughter kept talking about this Sparky—or Spark man— who was coming to her school. I finally said, "I'll go and show you that this guy could not help himself, let alone me." I called the school and got a little more information on the event. I was ready to bag me a fake Sparky man. I thought that he only wanted to go to her school to make money. Then I found out he was not charging anything. As I studied the group, I found that their whole mission was about being kind. I watched videos and read what I could. I even called a few schools where he had spoken previously and they said nothing but good things about this self-proclaimed recovering jerk.

I went to listen when he spoke the day he came to my daughter's school and found myself really listening to every word he said. When the program was over, I felt like a fan at a concert who wanted an autograph from a famous rock star.

When he was finished speaking with the kids, I stepped up to him, introduced myself, and asked if he had a few minutes to talk. I could tell that he really did not have any time to give me, but he asked if there was somewhere in town to get a Coke. We went to a little place, ordered our Cokes, and began to talk. I told him about myself, what I had gone through, and what I had put my family through over the last ten years. He said he needed to get something out of his car, and when he came back he had a diary filled with things he had done.

As we flipped through his book, he began to tell me that doing Sparks could help me with being depressed. He went on to give me the "I'm not a doctor speech" and told me to run everything he was saying by my doctor. He asked me to do five Sparks a day for the next thirty days. He went on to say, "For every Spark you do, I want you to write it down in a journal. I also want you to write down how doing that Spark made you feel and how you thought the other person felt."

He gave me 500 Spark cards and said that he needed me to commit to doing Sparks for thirty days. I promised him for thirty days I would make sure to do five Sparks a day. Dave then told me that I could only use money on half of the Sparks and the other half I had to do things that did not involve money. When I looked down at my watch, I realized that we had been talking for over an hour.

Dave said that he wanted me to understand two things. The first one was that, to some people, I am their entire world. He went on to explain that my children and husband needed me more that I would ever know or could imagine. The second thing he wanted me to understand was the pain I would cause the ones I loved if I committed suicide. He explained the feelings that he experiences every day because his father took his own life. He said, "There isn't a day that goes by that it does not hurt my heart." He told me that I may think my final actions will stop the pain and suffering, but what committing suicide does is cause a chain reaction of pain and destruction instead.

Dave got up, gave me a hug, and told me that he would send me a text every day to see how I was doing. That was over two years ago, and he has not failed to send a text every day. I am still doing five Sparks a day and that it has helped me so much that I am back to work and enjoying life so much. No, I am not trying to tell you that I do not struggle, but what I am saying is that I am so much better because One Spark took the time to teach me the value of doing Sparks. I am a life saved by One Spark.

LOVE SAVES – WOULD HAVE EVENTUALLY KILLED HERSELF

"For I will forgive their wickedness and will remember their sins no more." Hebrews 8:12 (NIV)

I have to tell you that I am fifteen years old and have made a lot of poor decisions in the past. I got to where I was very unhappy and had made the decision that I wanted to die. My childhood has been rotten and my mother has been doing drugs and alcohol my whole life. I've been taking drugs and drinking for about three years and that is how I have gotten through this thing called life.

I have had sex with three people and thought that was what love was all about. You came to speak at my school and it seemed as though you were speaking directly to me. I wanted to get up and leave because I thought someone had told you about me. I just sat and listened to your every word. After you spoke, I made my way down to talk to you, and you were very nice. I asked for a minute of your time and you gave me five minutes. People were coming up to speak to you and you asked them to wait. For the first time I felt like someone really cared about me and my situation. I told you what was going on with me, and you asked if I thought my parents would mind if we spoke. You told me to get a permission slip signed by them. They signed it.

We began to talk and you told me that I meant a lot to many people and that the world is a much better place because I was in it. You told me about the difference between chance and choice in life. We could not control who our family was but we could choose our future. We texted every day and you sent me a letter once a week to see how I was doing. Through our conversations I began to realize that the path I was on was not a good one and I needed to make a change.

I stopped drinking, doing drugs, and having sex. I am writing this letter to let everyone know how powerful One Spark is and what an angel you are.

I am here to tell you that I would have killed myself if it was not for Dave and One Spark. So if you are looking for someone and something to support—what better place than the place that taught me the value of my life and the choices I make.

A child alive because of love and kindness!

ONE MAN! MORE MEN? THIRTE
LYING, AND TAKING DRUGS

"Honor your father and moth
the Lord your God is giving you

Dave doesn't like his na
Spark exists because of his ..
year-old whose life has been forever changed because of one man.
We all have the power to help. Whether we do or not is our choice.

Hi! I am thirteen and I want to tell you that I have had a hard life
already because of my choices. I chose to smoke pot and drink. The
one thing I was never able to do was put my choices into consequences,
until David spoke at our school.

I sat there the day he came to our school and listened. At times
I felt like he knew everything I had been doing and was speaking
directly to me. I thought he would be like all the other people who
had been to our school and would try to do some magic or tell a lot
of jokes. I could not have been more wrong because he started right
in with choices that kids make and had a story of someone and the
consequences that had happened to them. I was not sure I believed
him, so after our assembly I went and asked if I could look a few
things up that David spoke about. My teacher said that I could, as
long as I shared the information with the class.

I told my teacher that I would, and then I set out to prove all
that he said wrong. But what I found was that he was dead on and if
I wanted a good job, I needed to make some changes. I went home
and asked my mom if she had time to talk and she said she did. I told
her about One Spark and what I had learned. I also told her that if
I didn't change, I would never get a good job and would never have
the life I wanted.

I told her that I would no longer lie, steal, drink, do drugs, or
cause her heartache anymore. Then I sent David a letter and told him
what I had decided, and he told me that I could do or be anything in

the world I wanted, I he want me to tell me how proud he was, and he said if he had a son, he would want him to be like me

My mom and dad are divorced, and I have not seen my father in a long time. David told me that I should not worry about my dad being absent, but I needed to focus on what is great about I love. I told him that I would do that. I write my mom a note every day and tell her how much I love her and how lucky I am to have a mom like her. She was gone shopping one day and I wanted to do a Spark for her, so I started to clean the house. I went into her room to dust and found a book that was titled, *The Best Gifts Ever.* I opened it up and my little notes were in this book. It has been two years since David spoke at my school, so you know there were a lot of notes.

I have not been in any trouble for over two years, and I have not broken my promise to my mom about not drinking and smoking pot. David, if I could choose a dad, I would want one like you!

THE ONE MAN – ONE SPARK CONSTRUCTION

"John answered, 'Anyone who has two shirts should share with the one who has none, and anyone who has food should do the same.'" Luke 3:11 (NIV)

There is a homeless man that lives in Wichita, Kansas, who has often asked for extra food, clothes, and other things that we hand out to give to others. I often wondered if he was telling me the truth, or if he just needed more. Well, I have to tell you that I really feel like a donkey because I ran into him one night when it was really cold and he was handing out sandwiches and giving out warm clothes he had received from us. I looked at him and said, "I have to tell you a story." And he said, "No you don't, because if you did not question, I would question your leadership."

I looked at his clothes and noticed they were not very warm. So I asked him what size boots he wore and he replied, "Eight." I said to him, "It is your lucky day, because I have these Sorel boots and I want to give them to you, but only if you do not give them away." I also had a pair of Columbia hunting coveralls and a Columbia hunting jacket. Again, I told him that he could have them, although he couldn't give away my gift, along with my hunting hat and full face mask hat.

It started to get cold for me, and I only had on a pair of sneakers and a thin jacket. I talked for about thirty more minutes with him and his friends until my body could not take any more.

As I started to drive off, I noticed a man who was walking, and he looked very cold. All I had was my scarf and hat that was given to me by a Spark Giver, and I pulled up next to him and asked if he wanted them. He said, "You are the One Spark dude, right?" And I said, "Yes." He asked if he could sit in the truck for a minute. Then he said he had a story to tell me and asked if I remembered him. At first I did not.

He said, "Last winter I was walking down Broadway when this man pulled up and asked where I was going, and I told him I was headed to a warm place to sleep. The man asked me when the last time I had slept in a bed was, and I told him a long time ago. The man offered to take me to a hotel and give me money for food. I told him—" I stopped him there because I suddenly remembered him. This man went on to say, "I told you not to give me money because I would just buy drugs with it. And you said to me, 'Not with this money, because it is a gift from my heart to yours.'"

The homeless man went on to tell me that he had not done drugs since that day. I asked him where he was going to sleep, and he said, "In my own bed." He has his own house and a job. He is a very good carpenter. This man told me that, the next day after we met, he called his parents and asked if he could talk to them. His mom and dad walked in the room he was in and he told them that he would never do drugs again and he wanted to start working, but he needed to borrow some money. They told him that they would have to think about it.

The next day he went to their house—clean. His dad told him that if he was still clean at the end of the week, he would loan him the money. He said, "I borrowed the money and have paid it all back.

I hire guys off of the streets to help me. I called my company One Spark Construction."

He said he had to run but needed to tell me something first. "I am the one." I asked, "What?" He replied, "You always said if there is one person you have touched, it would all be worth it. I am the one, and what you are doing is making a difference."

He stepped out of my truck and told me that he loved me. I sat there and cried for a while before I went home.

ONLY IN SIXTH GRADE – HAVING SEX AND SMOKING POT

"The Lord appeared to us in the past, saying: 'I have loved you with everlasting love; I have drawn you with unfailing kindness.'" Jeremiah 31:3 (NIV)

I am a sixth grader at a small school and have been smoking pot and having sex with a boy. After hearing One Spark (David) speak at our school about choices, it made me stop and think about my choices and what my life would be like in ten years. It made me sad to think of how many guys I might have been with and what drugs I might be doing then. I want to have a good future, and One Spark said to all of us that if we want to have a good life, we must be making good choices.

I have not been making good choices, and I wanted to make an excuse for my poor choices, but after listening to David Hill's story, I know I really have no excuse.

I love all the people on the One Spark page, and I will tell you that it is very important for you to post your stories because your stories give people hope that they can change. I love all of the love and kindness on this page. I was very depressed before I got here and started to read all the things that people are doing for others. Each one of you who think you don't make a difference, I want to tell you that you are wrong because you have made a difference in my life.

I will not smoke pot anymore, and I will not have sex again until

I am married. One Spark, thank you for what you have taught me. And to all of you, thank you for all the love and prayers I know you will send my way.

Miss Wrong to Miss Right.

ONE LIFE CHANGED, ONE LIFE SAVED – GIRL IN MEXICO NAMES SON DAVID

"For it is by grace you have been saved, through faith – and this is not from yourselves, it is a gift of God." Ephesians 2:8 (NIV)

Hi! I am a sixteen-year-old girl who lives in Mexico. I have been having sex with a boy and got pregnant, and I wanted to get rid of my baby. My parents work for the government and have good jobs, and I was scared of what they would say and that they would be ashamed of me. I also did not want to have a baby in this world that is so full of hate and greed.

One day I stumbled upon the One Spark Facebook page while at school. Soon I found myself going to this page several times a day. I saw that there were over 9,000 (568,000 now) who want the world to be nicer and more loving. I read what Mr. David said one day about children being the greatest gift that we will ever be given. I read all the posts from everyone and started to feel good about this world again.

I went to the doctor to make an appointment. Mr. David said that every action has a consequence. He went on to say that when we think a bad situation can't be fixed, we need to look at all the possibilities and see what great things may come our way.

This was sixteen months ago. I have to tell each of you that say you want to keep what you do between you and God that there are two lives that have been changed because of Mr. David and all the One Spark angels. You see, if you all would not have been posting your Sparks, I would have had an abortion. I am not here to debate if it is right or wrong, but you made me change my mind and keep my baby boy. You all are aunts and uncles!

Please keep us in your prayers and thoughts. One last thing to you all: POST YOUR SPARKS because you changed my life and allowed me to experience motherhood!

UPDATE ON LITTLE DAVID

Hi, David, and all of the One Spark angels. Today is little David's birthday. He is seven years old and is a good boy. A lot has happened since I last wrote to you. David, I know we have spoken a lot, but I wanted to write and let all of little David's aunts and uncles on this page know what is happening with us.

David is a great boy, very funny and smart. I have one more year of college and then I will have my degree in nursing. I will be twenty-three soon, and I still come to this page daily to get my love and kindness.

I again want to thank all of you who have prayed for me and little David in the past, and ask that you continue to pray for us.

David and One Spark, I want to thank you for all the help you have provided us, all of these years. It has made going to college possible.

FAMILY IS EVERYTHING – DYING CHILD WITH DOWN SYNDROME

"Behold, children are a gift of the Lord, The fruit of the womb is a reward." Psalm 127:3 (KJV)

I have to tell you about my daughter, Michelle, who has Down syndrome. She does function at a very high level. From a very early age she has been loving and a big giver. We have six children and she falls right in the middle. The stress and strain of having to focus on and care for Michelle caused some of our other kids to feel as though they did not get the attention they needed; my husband and I feel they are probably right.

Michelle has tried to keep the family together by calling them and inviting all of them home. All of our other children are out of college and working. She would call them every week and tell them that she loved them. We feel that they embrace her but would never fully connect with her because they never really had much to do with her as they were growing up.

My oldest son and Michelle did become close and talked every day. She told him one day that she was sad and he asked why. She told him that she felt like she was the cause of the family not being close. He told her that it was not her fault and that we all have choices in life, and each child made a choice not to stay close.

About a month later, Michelle became sick and went to the hospital with heart complications. I called all of my children and told them that the doctors did not think she would make it and they needed to come home because she had a massive heart attack. The next day, all of my kids were home and Michelle asked to speak to each one of them individually. As each one of them came out of her room, they were crying and upset. When my last child came out of Michelle's hospital room, she asked all of us to return to it together.

She showed me and my husband the contract Michelle had a nurse write up; each of our children signed it. Here is what the contract said:

I love all of you very much but you make me mad because family is everything, and all of you have nothing because you are not close. You promise to call each other two times a week and you promise to call mom and dad every day to tell them you love them. I want you to look up One Spark and be like all the Spark Givers on that page. My mom reads to me every day about what they are doing, and I want you to promise me you will be one.

Michelle loved to read the One Spark page every day. I am sad to say that Michelle passed away, and she told me before she died that she wished she could have been a better daughter and we could be proud of her like we are the other kids. I looked her in the eyes and told her that she has done more than all of the other kids combined. All of our kids got time with her and they told her how proud of her they were. She told them she never had a job or went to college, but my son told her that she had a Ph.D. in love and kindness.

The day of her funeral, Michelle wore the One Spark shirt David had given her. We love One Spark, Dave, and all of the other Spark angels.

Mom of Michelle.

JUST A MEAL? NO, STOPPED A SUICIDE

"For I was hungry and you gave me something to eat, I was thirsty and you gave me something to drink, I was a stranger and you invited me in." Matthew 25:35 (NIV)

There was a family of four eating at a restaurant I was in earlier tonight. I told my waiter that I wanted to buy the family's meal but to please not tell them who did it. After the family had left the restaurant, the waiter came over and said he had a message for me. He told me the lady and her family had just found out that she had breast cancer. She told the waiter to tell whoever did this that she had felt like committing suicide and to tell them thank you.

DADDY'S LITTLE GIRL – ARE YOU HONORING YOUR FATHER?

"Children, obey your parents in the Lord, for this is right. 'Honor your father and mother' – which is the first commandment with a promise 'so that it may go well with you and that you may enjoy long life on the earth.'" Ephesians 6:1–3 (NIV)

I was sixteen and had been in a lot of trouble for a few years after my dad passed away. My dad and I were very close, and when he died I felt like I had been left to face the world by myself. My mother and I have never been very close—maybe because we are so much alike—and I was daddy's little girl.

After my dad died, I started to do things to suppress my pain and make me feel better. I started looking for love in all the wrong places and had many partners. To make matters worse, I got pregnant and then lost the baby. I had been in trouble with the law and went to court for the eleventh time; the judge told me he was going to send me away for a long time if I came back.

I had missed a lot of school, but one Friday I woke up and decided to go since I hadn't been in a week. Little did I know this would be the day that would change my life! I was in math class, and a friend asked me what I thought this One Spark thing was all about, and I said that I didn't know anything about them.

I started to get up and leave, but for some reason I stayed. It was time for this big deal, and they pushed us into the gym like we were cattle. I was looking for who I thought would be the speaker and decided it had to be one of the ladies standing with this man in shorts. Wrong! The speaker was the man in shorts and flip flops. Our principal introduced him to us, and he started to tell us a little about himself. Then he told us his topic was called choices.

When he started talking about choices, I thought someone had told him about me because his talk seemed to be all about me. He asked the girls, "Can I talk to you for a minute?" Then he started telling us several stories about girls that had gotten AIDS and how terrible a death they had. He went on to say, "If one of these boys ever says to you, 'If you love me, you will do it,' look them straight in the eye and tell them, 'If you love me, you will not ask me to do something that I don't want to do.' "

Well, he laid it on us pretty thick, and I felt like crying but did not want the other kids to see me cry. So I walked down and spoke to a lady that was with Dave; her name was Alice. We talked for a little bit and then Dave was done. I told him why I had been doing the things that I had been doing and he said he was sorry for my loss, but I needed to quit using my dad as an excuse and start honoring him with my life. Alice jumped in and asked Dave to stop, but Dave looked at Alice and said that if I did not change my life soon, I would wind up in jail or dead. Dave walked over and gave me a hug and asked me this question. "If your dad was alive, would you be doing what you are doing now?" I stood there for what seemed like a year and said, "No."

Dave told me that he could sense I had great things that I could do with my life. Alice stepped up and asked if she could chat with me for a minute. She told me that her life before David got ahold of her was just like mine. I asked her to tell me more and she did. We sat there for over an hour, and the last thing Alice told me was that I had very little time to change and needed to make a decision very soon. She told me not to follow in her footsteps and wait until life was no longer worth living. We hugged and then I walked over to Dave and said thank you for caring and all the love. He gave me his email address and then gave me a hug and said that he loved me.

I started to cry and he said to me, "Don't look back but only look forward." I left school that day feeling for the first time that everything was going to be okay. When I got home, my mom and I talked and cried for hours and then I told her about One Spark and what they did. We have stayed in touch with One Spark. To every principal or administrator in the world, if you have not had One Spark in yet, you need to give them a call NOW and let them have a chance to reach out to the kids who have given up on life like I did.

I am now in college, and I am going to be a doctor so I can give back. Dave always said that all he needed to know is that if there was one life changed, it would make it all worth it. My friend, count my life as a life changed.

Daddy's Little Girl

Forgiveness – Lost Only Child and Husband to Drunk Driver Who Just Lost His Family

"For as high as the heavens are above the earth, so great is his love for those who fear him; as far as the east is from the west, so far has he removed our transgressions from us." Psalm 103:11–12 (NIV)

I am a very private person and have really never believed that we should talk about what we do to help other people, because our rewards are in heaven. I no longer believe this way—not that our rewards are in heaven—but that our stories can help others.

About seven months ago, I lost my only child and husband due to a drunk driving accident. My husband had to pick up our daughter from work. It was around 10 PM on a Friday night. They were almost home when a car slammed into them, killing my husband on impact. My daughter was trapped in the car and it took over two hours to get her out.

I was at home when a friend called and said there had been an accident and I needed to get there right away. When I arrived, the police tried to pull me away, but I pushed right through and when I got to the car, I knew my husband was dead and I knew my little girl would not make it. I asked the fireman if I could hold her hand and talk to her and he said yes. About two hours into this nightmare, I could sense that she was not going to make it. I told her that I loved her and my life was blessed because she was there. She said to me that she loved me, and then she said the strangest thing. She said, "You have to forgive this person and use my death for a greater purpose." I looked at her and said, "Okay."

She died in the car before they could get her out. Imagine my horror when I looked over and saw a young man being pulled out of his car and, to my surprise, he looked as though he had no injuries. I started to scream at him and call him all kinds of names. I really do not remember much after that.

A policeman drove me home, and it seemed as though the next few days were a blur. I had my family here to help make the arrangements for the funerals. My mom and dad were here the next day. My father is a preacher and my mom is the kindest lady that I have ever met. After the funerals, I started talking to my dad about what had happened, and he told me that I needed to be thankful that God blessed me with the time that I had with my husband and daughter. He went on to tell me that I might have a broken heart but at least we know that their final resting spot is in heaven.

My father took a leave of absence from the church to help me get everything done. About three months after their deaths, I woke up and saw my husband and my daughter before me. They both said that if I am unwilling to forgive this person, then I will wear this ball and chain called hate for the rest of my life. I have never come to grips with whether I saw them or dreamed of them, but either way I know that God sent them. It was 3 AM and I went into where my mom and dad were supposed to be sleeping, only to find them wide awake. I told them I had something to say and they said they did also. For you see, that night we were all visited by angels, and we were all told that we needed to forgive and move on.

My dad told me that the amount of hate he had in his heart for this person was tremendous. He said, "Not only did he take my only grandchild, but he took one of my very best friends." We all agreed that night that we would go see this man the next day.

We went to the jail and asked if we could see him, and they said they would ask him. Before the officer went to ask the man, he turned to us and said, "Please go easy on him because he has tried to commit suicide twice since he was arrested." We met in a jail room, and when he walked in, I realized he was only a boy. We began to speak with him to find out what happened and he told us his story.

"I just turned seventeen last week," he said. I replied, "This must be hard on your parents," and he said, "No, because they are both dead. I lost my father in the war, and my mother had just passed away from breast cancer the night that this happened." He went on to tell us how sorry he was, and that he did not want to live because of what he had done. What came out of my mouth shocked me when I said, "I forgive you, and we do love you."

We talked for over two hours, and when we got ready to leave, I said to him, "You cannot commit suicide because we have to make sure that my family did not die in vain."

We went to his court date and think we shocked everyone when we were called as defense witnesses. I told them that we did not want him to do jail time, but he needed to use his life for good. We continued with saying to them, "We feel that when you look at this young man's history, you will find that he had never been in trouble." As I walked by him to go to my seat, I leaned over and gave him a hug. I said to him, "This is the kind of love that God has for us, and you need to show this to everyone that you meet."

He was sentenced to three years; we write to each other a lot. I have told him that when he gets out, I will be here to help him get his life back in order.

This is a little note from him to every kid out there who doesn't believe that this could happen to them. "I have killed two people, and that will haunt me for the rest of my life. I now have a felony on my record and this will keep me from getting a job. I will lose over four years of my life—which is nothing to being killed. DO NOT DRINK AND DRIVE because it will ruin your life and the lives of many other people."

—A mom who lost it all and who has been given a chance to understand what God's pure love is all about.

Not Hungry Anymore – Groceries Bought For Family Who Lost Job

"And if you spend yourselves in behalf of the hungry and satisfy the needs of the oppressed, then your light will rise in the darkness, and your night will become like noonday." Isaiah 58:10 (NIV)

Hi, One Spark!

I was in Walmart trying to get some stuff for my family, and it was very few things since my husband and I both have lost our jobs. I handed the gal my credit card and it was declined. I handed her another one and it was declined also. I started to feel sweat running down my forehead, and I became very embarrassed!

That is when a man walked up and handed the cashier his credit card and said he would pay for my groceries! I started to cry uncontrollably, and he gave me a hug and told me everything was going to be okay. He started to talk to me and asked me why I was only getting a few things, and this is when I told him that my husband and I lost our jobs, due to economic downturn at our company.

He told the young lady working the register that we'd be right back; he asked her not to ring up my items just yet. He said to me, "Come on, let's get the things your family needs." I begged him not to take me back into the store, for I was figuring this was some kind of joke! I told him that we had four children, who were the love of our lives, and it was killing us not to be able to provide the things they love to eat!

Pretty soon we filled up one shopping cart and then another. I know he offered to pay, but still all the way there my heart was pounding—thinking that this man was going to walk away when we got to the front of the register! He did pay for everything; the bill came to $475. I began to cry and cry, the lady behind me began to cry, the girl ringing up all of the food began to cry, and as I looked around, most people near us were crying as well.

The man helped carry the groceries out to my car, gave me a hug and a kiss on the cheek, and told me he loved me. I just happened to look up as he drove off in a pink truck. I did not know that Jesus rode in a pink truck, but surely he must! This has renewed my faith in humanity and the love of Jesus Christ!

The man gave me a One Spark card, and I could not wait to get home to check out what this organization was all about. I am amazed at what this group does to make the world a better place.

Thank you again to the man in the pink truck. You have made it easier for us to get through the next few months with food in our cabinets. I promise when we're back on our feet, we will pass on the Spark you gave us!

FATHER AND SON TOGETHER AGAIN AND NEW BABY ON THE WAY

"Grandchildren are the crown of the aged, and the glory of children is their fathers." Proverbs 17:6 (ESV)

This was written to One Spark:

I am fairly new to this website, but I found myself drawn to opening up the One Spark page in the morning and several times throughout the day. The last thing I did right before I went to bed was read all the posts. I then lay down with a smile on my face. I wanted to do a Spark right away and wondered who I could Spark. Then it hit me that my son and I have not talked in over a year. It really doesn't matter why, but what matters is that we were both stubborn and would not budge.

I read a post from Dave about friends and how sometimes we need to be more concerned with friendship than being right. So, I called my son and he did not answer. He lives two hours away, so I got up early on Saturday and headed to my son's house. I arrived there at around 7 AM and knocked on the door. When my son opened the door, he asked if everything was all right. I said no and asked if I could come in. I could see he was worried that something might have happened to his mom or sister. Then I told him they were fine, but I wanted to tell him I was sorry for how I have treated him in the past. Again he asked me if I was all right. I told him that I had missed him so much and that I wanted him back in my life.

We were both crying, which woke his wife up. When she came in the room and saw us hugging and crying, she began to cry also. She asked both of us to sit down and told us that this was the happiest day of her life. Then she went on to tell me and my son that she was pregnant and so relieved that their baby's grandparents were going to be a part of its life.

We all jumped into the car and headed to my house to tell my wife the news. When we walked in together, my wife broke down into tears. I told her what I did, and she told me that this was the reason she married me. Then we told her about the baby and she started to cry again. If anyone doubts that One Spark works, I will set them straight. If it had not been for this site, I still would not be talking to my son. I love One Spark because it did start a fire within me.

Prove Who Wrong? – Lady Lost Her Son in War

"In everything I did, I showed you that by this kind of hard work we must help the weak, remembering the words the Lord Jesus himself said: 'It is more blessed to give than to receive.'" Acts 20:35 (NIV)

I have been on your page for a long time and have read the stories. To be honest, I felt as though either you were paying these people to post or they were all made up. I would sit at the dinner table and tell my family what a fraud you guys were and that I was disgusted with all this garbage. My eighteen-year-old daughter told me one night that the only way I was ever going to know if this Spark stuff was legitimate or not was to do my own study. Then my whole family started in on me and told me to put my money where my mouth was.

So, I told them that I would write and get some of these cards and I would prove that Spark giving didn't really matter to the world or anybody. I got my cards, and I went out one day and bought a lady a cup of coffee and she asked, "Why?" I told her I was trying to prove that Spark giving does not make a difference to anyone. She asked what a Spark giver was and I told her. What she said next shook me at my foundation and made me think. She said, "You may think you only bought me a cup of coffee, but you did much more than that for me. I lost my son in the war and have felt alone for seven years, and your Spark warmed my heart and made me realize that my son did not die in vain. This world was worth fighting for and it gave me strength to move forward one more day."

I talked to this lady for over two hours and we took turns buying meals for people at McDonald's; we did seventeen Sparks. When we got ready to leave, we hugged and cried and told each other that this

Spark giving is the real deal. I have to admit that I was wrong and will continue to be a Spark Giver until the day I die.

Love, A true Spark Giver convert.

P.S. Never think that your Sparks are small, because to someone else they are very big.

Story of Forgiveness – Parents of Daughter Forgive Man Who Murdered Her

"For if you forgive other people when they sin against you, your heavenly Father will also forgive you. But if you do not forgive others their sins, your Father will not forgive your sins." Matthew 6:14–15 (NIV)

I wanted to send you a Spark that I gave to the man who murdered my daughter—not with a gun, but by supplying her with drugs for sex.

My daughter was the All-American girl. She was a good student, athlete, and a great daughter. She was the daughter every mother would have loved to be blessed with in life. Kerry was so beautiful that every boy wanted to date her. However, she was not into dating; she was concerned with her grades because she wanted to be a doctor. And I knew one day she would be one.

Kerry asked me if she could go to a party her junior year and I said yes, as I had no worries that she would do anything wrong. I told her she had to be home at 11 PM. When 11:00 came and went, I got worried and called her phone. There was no answer. Her dad and I went to go look for her but couldn't find her. She finally came home at 2 AM. She didn't act right, but we let her go to bed and told her that we would deal with the situation in the morning.

She did not wake up until around three that afternoon, and when we started to talk to her, she became mean and nasty. She yelled at us for the first time ever. We were shocked and could not believe that this was our daughter. She only got worse, and we suspected she was on drugs, but she would never admit it. We had her tested and, sure enough, she failed for meth. We were shocked, scared, and mad all at the same time.

We tried everything and then my husband started to ask her friends who she was seeing. They told us and we confronted him. Of course, he denied knowing where she would be getting the drugs and told us that he loved her and would do anything for her.

Months passed and Kerry became worse. One night we received a call from our local police chief, and he told us that we needed to come to see him. We have been friends with him for over twenty-five years. He told us that our daughter had died of a heroin overdose. She was only seventeen.

They arrested her boyfriend who had heroin in him; he was higher than a kite. He was charged with her death and sentenced to seven years in prison. Three years into his sentence, my husband and I went to see him and told him that we forgave him for what he did to our daughter.

When he came up for parole, we went to the hearing and asked that he be shown mercy. The board did, but before they made their decision, the members asked us why. We told them that we read many Sparks of forgiveness on the One Spark page. We gave them each a One Spark card and they proceeded to meet in order to reach a decision. When they came back, they said they looked at both the website and Facebook page and now understood why we felt the way we did, but they were not sure they could have made that same decision.

They let the young man out of prison. He has been clean and is in college. He is doing well and we are proud of him. People ask us how and why, and we answer by saying, "Look at what Jesus did for us when we were sinners." And then we add, "We all have something to offer the world to make it a better place. The only question is— will we?"

STUCK AND DRUNK – STAR ATHLETE CAREER ENDED – BECAME YOUTH PASTOR

"Do not boast about tomorrow, for you do not know what a day may bring." Proverbs 27:1 (NIV)

I do not know where to begin, so I will jump in head first. I have been a drunk for some time—who am I kidding—all of my adult life. I was a great high school athlete and had scholarships to a lot of colleges. I blew out my knee in the last game I played in, and the doctor said it was so bad that I would not be able to play sports anymore. I never had a backup plan, because I knew I was going to college and then on to the pros. When I received the news that I was done playing sports, I was done with life.

I had been dating the same girl since I was in the seventh grade, and she told me not to worry about it and that everything would be all right. My girlfriend was a great Christian and lived what she believed. This meant, for me, no sex before marriage. I loved her so much that it was not a big deal. She went on to college, became a physician assistant, and then came back home to work in our home town. We got married—and trust me—everyone told her not to marry a drunk like me, but she would tell them that God was going to change me. When we got married, I got worse and worse in the drinking game. I got a DUI, and then everyone, including my own parents, told my wife to leave me. She told them all that this is not what God wanted her to do. She stuck by me, even when I hit bottom by getting into a wreck with a girl in my truck. The rumors that I was having affair started to fly. Before God, I have never had an affair. I was drunk, so this was my second DUI. I was to be sentenced in three weeks.

My wife asked me what I wanted to do with my life. I said that I wanted to change, but life was hard, and I could not get over it. She told me about the One Spark Foundation and the guy who started it. She told me that his life, as a child, sucked. She also told me that he had a way to help me move on, if I would only let him help me. I told her that I would contact him on Wednesday. Later, when she asked me if I had called him, I told her that I had, but he never returned my call. She said, "That is weird, because he said he had not heard from you." I replied, "Well, there must be a problem with his phone." My wife then surprised me by saying, "That is why he came here to see you."

I sat there for a moment and asked, "He what?" She told me that he was outside and he wanted to talk to me. I went outside and he was standing by his truck. I said, "Hi" and he said, "Hi." Then the conversation took a turn that I was not comfortable with. He asked me why I was holding on to my football days. I told him that I was supposed to go to college and then on to the NFL. He looked at me and then asked for the contract that I had signed between me and God. Then he said, "Oh, you don't have one, right?" I answered, "No, I do not have a contract!" He just sat there with a dumb look on his face, which turned into a huge smile. He told me his story, and I have to admit that I wanted to cry but did not want to give him the power. We talked a lot about my anchor and how I could turn it into a key. He spent a lot of time with me, and then he told me that if I didn't change, I could lose the thing that I loved the most in the world.

Dave drove five hours just to speak with me. I was rude, mean, and very hateful, even after hearing what he went through as a child. I didn't want to hear anything at all he had to say.

The last thing he told me was that I must not have been a very good football player, because I was a limp dick. I said, "What?!" He continued with, "Stop feeling sorry for yourself. Start by counting your blessings. Begin with being thankful for your wife who never left you. She never cheated on you. Do you know there are several guys, including doctors, who have wanted to go out with her? But she loves only you." Then he told me to think back to when I played football, and how I would put every ounce of energy I had into winning. Dave reminded me that I had a great Christian wife, faithful friend, and a soon-to-be mother. Again, I replied with, "What?!" He said she had told him about her pregnancy and that Dave could give me the news that I was going to be a father. I do not know why, but I started to cry.

Dave told me that he had to go, gave me a hug, and then gave my wife a hug and told both of us that he loved us and so did Jesus. I held my wife and made a promise to her that I would never touch a drop of alcohol again. That was six years ago, and I have never touched a drop of alcohol since that date. I went back to college and became a youth pastor.

I use what I learned from Dave to help many kids. I recently had a conversation with a young man, similar to the one Dave had with me. He sat there and then told me that he did not believe the story. I got Dave on the phone, who laid it out the only the way he could. I then asked this young man whether he was a man or a mouse. The youngster said that he was a man, and then Dave replied, "Then stop acting like a mouse and take control of your life." Dave told him that he loved him and would see him soon. As I looked at this fellow, I saw he had tears in his eyes, and so did I. I have changed many young kids' hearts with the stories I have lived and the stories I have learned from Dave. To date, we have taken several hundred kids off the streets where we live—and no, it is not in my home town. We moved to a big city, with a high crime rate and a high incarceration rate of children.

Thank you, Dave, One Spark, and everyone on this page who care about kids. You see, my kids do not believe that you care about them, so please show them some love.

WISH-GRANTING FAIRY IN THE SKY – SAID WHAT NEEDS TO BE SAID

"I am not saying that I am in need, for I have learned to be content in whatever circumstances. I know what it is to be in need, and I know what it is to have plenty. I have learned the secret of being content in any and every situation, whether well fed or hungry, whether living in plenty or in want. I can do all this through him who gives me strength." Philippians 4:11–13 (NIV)

I was on the phone with a good friend the other day. After

covering important topics, like disparaging each other's mothers and retelling semi-factual tales from our college days, our conversation turned to the mundane.

"So, how's work going?" he asked.

For those of you who don't know, I make money by teaching leadership skills and helping people learn to get along in corporate America. My wife says it's all a clever disguise so I can get up in front of large groups and tell stories.

I plead the fifth.

I answered my buddy's question with, "Definitely feeling blessed. Last year was the best year yet for my business. And it looks like this year will be just as busy." The words rolled off my tongue without a second thought—like reciting the Pledge of Allegiance or placing my usual lunch order at McDonald's.

But it was a lie.

Now, before you start taking up a collection for the "Feed the Dannemillers" fund, allow me to explain. Based on last year's quest to go twelve months without buying anything, you may have the impression that our family is subsisting on Ramen noodles and free chips and salsa at the local Mexican restaurant. Not to worry, we are not in dire straits.

Last year was the best year yet for my business.

But that is not a blessing.

I've noticed a trend among Christians, myself included, and it troubles me. Our rote response to material windfalls is to call ourselves blessed—like the "Amen" at the end of a prayer.

"This new car is such a blessing."

"Finally closed on the house. Feeling blessed."

"Just got back from a mission trip. Realize how blessed we are here in this country."

On the surface, the phrase seems harmless. Faithful even. Why wouldn't I want to give God the glory for everything I have? Isn't that the right thing to do?

No.

As I reflected on my "feeling blessed" comment, two thoughts came to mind. I realize I'm splitting hairs here, creating an argument over semantics. But bear with me, because I believe it is critically important. It's one of those things we can't see because it's so culturally engrained that it has become normal.

But it has to stop. And here's why.

First, when I say that my material fortune is the result of God's blessing, it reduces The Almighty to some sort of sky-bound, wish-granting fairy who spends his days randomly bestowing cars and cash upon his followers. I can't help but draw parallels to how I handed out M&M's to my own kids when they followed my directions and chose to poop in the toilet rather than in their pants. Sure, God wants us to continually seek His will, and it's for our own good. But positive reinforcement?

God is not a behavioral psychologist.

Second, and more importantly, calling myself blessed because of material good fortune is just plain wrong. For starters, it can be offensive to the hundreds of millions of Christians in the world who live on less than one dollar per day. You read that right. Hundreds of millions of people receive a single-digit dollar "blessing" per day.

During our year in Guatemala, Gabby and I witnessed, first-hand, the damage done by the theology of prosperity, where faithful people scraping by to feed their families were simply told they must not be faithful enough. If they were, God would pull them out of their nightmare. Just try harder, and God will show favor.

The problem? Nowhere in Scripture are we promised worldly ease in return for our pledge of faith. In fact, the most devout saints from the Bible usually died penniless, receiving a one-way ticket to prison or death by torture.

I'll take door number three, please.

If we're looking for the definition of blessing, Jesus spells it out clearly (Matthew 5: 1–12). (NIV)

[1] Now when Jesus saw the crowds, he went up on a mountainside and sat down. His disciples came to Him,

² And He began to teach them. He said:

³ Blessed are the poor in spirit, for theirs is the kingdom of heaven.

⁴ Blessed are those who mourn, for they will be comforted.

⁵ Blessed are the meek, for they will inherit the earth.

⁶ Blessed are those who hunger and thirst after righteousness, for they will be filled.

⁷ Blessed are the merciful, for they shall be shown mercy.

⁸ Blessed are the pure in heart, for they will see God.

⁹ Blessed are the peacemakers, for they will be called the sons of God.

¹⁰ Blessed are those who are persecuted because of righteousness, for theirs is the kingdom of heaven.

¹¹ Blessed are you when people insult you, persecute you and falsely say all kinds of evil against you because of me.

¹² Rejoice and be glad, because great is your reward in heaven, for in the same way they persecuted the prophets who were before you.

I have a sneaking suspicion that verses 12a, 12b, and 12c were omitted from the text. That's where the disciples responded by saying in 12a, "Waitest thou for one second, Lord. What about 'blessed art thou comfortable,' or in 12b, 'blessed art thou which havest good jobs, a modest house in the suburbs, and a yearly vacation to the Florida Gulf Coast?'"

12c: And Jesus said unto them, "Apologies, my brothers, but those did not maketh the cut."

So there it is. Written in red. Plain as day. Even still, we ignore it all when we hijack the word "blessed" to make it fit neatly into our modern American ideals, creating a cosmic lottery where every sincere prayer buys us another scratch-off ticket. In the process, we stand the risk of alienating those we are hoping to bring to the faith.

And we have to stop playing that game.

The truth is, I have no idea why I was born where I was or why I have the opportunity I have. It's beyond comprehension. But I certainly don't believe God has chosen me above others because of the veracity of my prayers or the depth of my faith. Still, if I take advantage of the opportunities set before me, a comfortable life may come my way. It's not guaranteed. But if it does happen, I don't believe Jesus will call me blessed.

He will call me "burdened."

He will ask,

"What will you do with it?"

"Will you use it for yourself?"

"Will you use it to help?"

"Will you hold it close for comfort?"

"Will you share it?"

So many hard choices. So few easy answers.

So my prayer today is that I understand my true blessing. It's not my house. Or my job. Or my standard of living.

No.

My blessing is this. I know a God who gives hope to the hopeless. I know a God who loves the unlovable. I know a God who comforts the sorrowful. And I know a God who has planted this same power within me—within all of us.

And for this blessing, may our response always be,

"Use me."

Since I had this conversation, my new response is simply, "I'm grateful." Would love to hear your thoughts.

SEVENTY-FOUR-YEAR-OLD GIVING SPARKS

"Behold, children are a heritage from the Lord, the fruit of the womb a reward." Psalm 127:3 (ESV)

I am seventy-four years old and have watched the world become worse and worse over the years. People used to stop and ask if you were all right, and if you were in trouble, they would lend a hand. Many people like me sit back and complain about how bad it has gotten, but do nothing to change it. I lost my husband seven years ago. He was my world, and I really did not want to go on, but I have six children and fifteen grandchildren. I wanted to be there for them, and in reality they were there for me.

One of my granddaughters is a sophomore in high school, and she had just heard the One Spark people speak. She was very excited to begin Sparking. Her mom and dad are very busy doctors, so she spends a lot of time with me. I am thankful for that, because without her, I would have lost my mind. She came to my house and told me about doing Sparks. I thought we were going to be lighting things on fire, not making people smile. She got on the web and found the One Spark page; we read the beginning story together and I cried.

I knew I wanted to do this, and I wanted to do it with my granddaughter. We made a plan and off we went to spread some Sparks. People were wondering what we were up to, and that broke my heart. It used to be that when someone did something kind, we said thank you and never questioned their motives. I guess with all the craziness in the world, we probably should question things.

We made thirty-dozen cookies and put them in bags with a One Spark card we printed from the web. People were so happy and thankful for the Sparks we gave, and a few people started to cry. I know they were not crying because of how good the cookies were, because I am no Betty Crocker at all. I think people just want to feel loved and appreciated.

We are planning our next mission to Spark people and hope to be out doing so soon. It has really helped my granddaughter and me connect and build a relationship. If you have kids or grandkids, I would recommend this Sparking, because it will build a wall of love.

I hope I made you smile with our Sparks.

SINGLE LADY IN SIXTIES – SPARK LEADS TO NEW COUPLE

"Rejoice in hope, be patient in tribulation, be constant in prayer."
Romans 12:12 (ESV)

Here is my Spark that I did. It is a little one, but I hope I make someone smile.

I am a single lady in my mid-sixties, and I have not been very social after my husband of forty-four years left me for another woman. I just went to work and then stayed in my home with my cat. I got to the point that I really did not like talking to anyone.

I got a new neighbor who was in his seventies, and he was very nice. I talked to him once and then he wanted to talk all the time. I felt like he was alone, since he lost his wife of fifty years. He was always outside when I got home from work, and we would talk a little bit. We did this for almost a year.

I had decided to retire at the end of the month and it was winter. Jack (my neighbor) fell and had to be rushed to the hospital. I guess he put me as his person to contact in an emergency. I arrived at the hospital as soon as I could. When I got there, I found out that Jack had fallen and broken his leg. I called work and told them that I was going to retire that day, so I could take care of Jack.

I cooked and cleaned for him, and he made a fast recovery. When he was well, he told me that he wanted to take me to see his farm. We left the next morning and spent four weeks there. I had to buy clothes and women things.

Jack and I are a couple now. He sure is my Spark, and he tells me I am his Spark. Jack sure has made me feel loved again, and I could never repay him for his love.

I hope this is a good Spark.

ARE YOU AN HONEST MAN? – RENEWED FAITH IN PEOPLE

"To do what is right and just is more acceptable to the Lord than sacrifice." Proverbs 21:3 (NIV)

I want to tell you about a Spark my family and I received while traveling to a new home. We moved to get a new job because there were none in the town where we lived. We were in Mississippi and our truck broke down. It was going to cost a lot of money we did not have. We had the truck towed to a mechanic's shop. He told us that we blew the transmission and it would need to be overhauled. The estimate was $1,735 and we did not have it. I started to cry because my husband had to be at work on Monday, or he would lose his job.

The man who owned the garage came and asked my husband if he was an honest man and he said yes. Then the man told my husband he was going to fix the truck and then we could pay him later. The owner fixed our truck, we did make it to our new town, and my husbanded did get the job. We sent the garage money every week and finally got the bill paid off. Then the craziest thing happened to us. When we made the last payment on the transmission a couple of weeks later, we got a check back from the owner and a note that said thank you for renewing my faith in people. He said in the note that he had helped many people over the years and none had paid him back. He went on to ask us to please use the money to help our family and then he thanked us.

We just sat there and cried. Then we knew we had to help someone else with the money. There is a man who works with my husband and needed his car worked on. I can't remember what needed to be done, but I know that they only had one car and it was impossible for them to get to where they needed to go. We called him up and told him we wanted to pay for his car to get fixed. I guess it was a van. It cost $682.73 to fix it, and they were so happy that they cried and told us that no one had ever helped them before.

We are still looking to help other people with the other money we got back from the owner of the garage. The One Spark page has reminded us that we need to help other people. We know that if we were not familiar with One Spark, we would have just blown that money on ourselves.

GRAB YOUR KEY

"Come to me, all who labor and are heavy laden, and I will give you rest. Take my yoke upon you, and learn from me, for I am gentle and lowly in heart, and you will find rest for your souls. For my yoke is easy, and my burden is light." Matthew 11:28-30 (ESV)

Today I need everyone to get their keys out and hold them in your hands. I want you to listen to these words very closely because they will show you how you will be able to use everything that has happened to you to benefit someone else.

Please know that every one of us has a key ring. Life constantly throws unfortunate circumstances our way—loss of a job, divorce, betrayal by a friend, loss of a child or loved one, bankruptcy, teenage pregnancy, someone cheating on you, someone gossiping about you, a horrible marriage, or a bad childhood.

God did not give us these bad situations, but His desire is to turn all the rotten things that have happened to us to his glory. "What?" you may ask…Yes, God has given us a key chain to place all the bad bumps in our life onto. He then wants us to realize that each of these keys can unlock the hearts, minds, and souls of someone else going through what we went through.

Don't be sad or complain about all the bad things that have happened to you. Instead, promise to use your heartache to help someone else. When we are sitting around and asking what we have to offer the world, reach into your pocket or purse and pull out your key chain of heartache and misery. Rename it as blessings and love for others. After you have renamed your key chain, USE IT for the glory of God and to the benefit of mankind. There are so many people who have gone through what we have experienced. We can lend them our knowledge, understanding, and love to get them through their situation much faster and without all the troubles we endured!

Today, grab your key chain of blessings and love and use it to benefit those who are hurting and feel as though they will never make it past their situation. Take their hand, show them that you have been where they are, and share with them what you had to do to get through your situation. Tell them that you will be there for them to lean on, and that when times get really bad, you will be there to help them up and to move on.

Love, David A2J

LOVE AND TIME – LEUKEMIA WAS HER KEY

"Even though I walk through the valley of the shadow of death, I will fear no evil, for you are with me; your rod and your staff, they comfort me." Psalm 23:4 (ESV)

Hi David and the One Spark board. I want to say thank you for helping my family in our time of need. To everyone on this page, here is what a great organization you are following and supporting.

My daughter fought leukemia for over nine years and lost her fight two months ago. David met her while speaking at her middle school about the power of kindness and the importance of making positive choices. She was in the middle of her chemo and had lost her hair.

There was an instant connection between Bethany and David. He would write her and call her at least once a week. There were many days David could tell that she was down, and he would make the effort to cheer her up. David would do whatever it took to get her to laugh.

There were many days she would call him just to tell him she loved him and that he was her hero. He would always tell her that he could not be her hero, because she was his hero.

My daughter got better for about three years and then the cancer came back worse than it was before. She made it her mission to Spark as many people as she could while she was on this earth.

David would make it to see her as often as he could. When she went back into the hospital, David made it a point to see her every day. They would laugh and would pull as many pranks as possible. This kept her spirits up and seemed to make her feel better each time he came up to see her.

When the time came to let her go to be with the Lord, David was right there to hold her hand and be a comfort to our family. Then a couple of other people started to come with David, and they were a blessing also.

I am a single mother who had not worked much in the last year, and when B died, I did not know how I was going to pay for the funeral. This is when One Spark stepped up and told me they would be paying the funeral expenses for my daughter. I just started to cry when I got the news.

Thank you, One Spark and David, for all you do to make the world a better place.

Family Tradition

"Do not cheat your neighbor. Do not rob him. Do not hold back the pay of a hired worker until morning." Leviticus 19:13 (NIRV) New International Reader's Version

Hi David and One Spark.

I am sixteen years old and wanted to start a fire in my town. Not a real fire, but a fire of kindness and love. I go to a large school that has many problems; a lot of people get picked on daily. I am not one of them because I come from money, am a good athlete, and am a cheerleader.

I do not think that any of the things I mentioned should put me above anyone else. My family members are very wealthy and have generous hearts. My father took over the family business from his father, who was not a nice man. He used people to get what he wanted and never truly cared about people.

When my father bought his father out of the business, my mother told him that we, as a family, needed to sit down and take a look at how we planned to invest our money in the company. My father looked at my mother, who has a degree from the Wharton School of Business, and said, "I am not sure what you are talking about; this must be something you learned while at Wharton." My mother told him it was something she was taught by her family, who had nothing to offer except love.

My mother went on to tell my father that he needed to call a meeting with all the employees, and he needed to close the business on that day and pay them for their time. He also needed to cater food in and make this a party. When my mother puts her foot down, my dad just smiles and says, "Okay dear."

My father went to the managers and told them of his plan; many of them could not believe what he was saying. A lot of them had worked at this business for over twenty years and had never been given a party.

The festivities were all set, and my mother went into high gear. She planned it all, and it was going to be a party like no one had ever seen—for only the employees and their families.

On the day of the party, my mother and father greeted everyone. My mother had a lady by her side taking notes like her life depended on it. I was only thirteen, so I really never understood what was going on, until the next day when my mother told us kids we were going to help her bless the workers of our business.

My mother took the notes that the lady had taken for her and off we went in search of many items. There were seven of us kids and I was the third oldest. My mother was not one to mess with when she was on a mission, and all of us kids knew it.

Once we had found the things that were listed on the paper, my mother started to back order them, and we kids fell right in line. My mother was a stickler for being on time, and when she told these stores what time she wanted the purchased items to be delivered, they had better be early. Or they were in trouble.

They were delivered exactly when they were supposed to be—washing machines, beds, clothes, and many other things. It took four days to deliver all the stuff she bought for the employees, but she got it done. My father was worried about us going bankrupt and not having anything. My mother would not hear any of his nonsense, and she let my father know this.

This was happening in 1970, and times were a bit hard. The company made all kinds of products and needed to rethink how they were being manufactured. After my mother gave each employee what they had asked for, she again asked for a meeting to speak with them. My father thought she was going to give them more stuff. She told the employees what was going on and that she needed their help with product design, marketing, manufacturing, and every other part of this business. She went on to tell them that when the company made this money, they all would get a raise. She also told them that if the company lost money, they would lose pay.

The company took off, profits went through the roof, and the pay of the employees went up as well. The company now runs smoothly, and the employees will not put up with anyone messing around. They are the life blood of the company.

At ages eighty-one and eighty-two, my mother and father have long since retired, but they are still a part of the business. I have been running the business with my family for many years now, and we are grooming three of our children to take over the business from us.

I am not sure how I found this page, or if the page found me, but I would like to think that my mother started a fire of kindness in our company that will never be put out. I would like to think she is a Master Spark Giver. Our company prides itself on giving to those in need, and our employees give of their time, talent, and treasure every day.

Thank you for what you are doing and what you are teaching, because giving is a lost art. If we do not teach people today, one day it will not exist at all.

Living Nightmare – Sold For Sex – Goal to Help Educate

"If someone is caught kidnapping a fellow Israelite and treating or selling them as a slave, the kidnapper must die. You must purge the evil from among you." Deuteronomy 24:7 (NIV)

I want to first say thank you for helping me get free from the nightmare I was in and the abuse I suffered every day.

I was rebellious at a young age and made many poor decisions that eventually led me to be sold like a piece of meat, many times a day. I rebelled against the people who had me, and I found out that the consequences were not good for someone who did this, possibly leading to being beaten so bad that you only wished to die.

They used many different ways to keep me in line: drugs, beatings, and even threatening to take my little sister and selling her. I eventually gave up and gave in.

I would sleep with as many as fifteen men a day—I never saw a dime. These men would do things to me that even the worst horror show could not depict. I led a life of misery, and when a new man came in, he knew he could do whatever he wanted to me, and they would never say a word. The more perverted the men were, the more they would pay the people who held us captive.

I never in a million years thought that I would wind up in a place like this, having to do the most disgusting things you could imagine. It got so bad that I would try to kill myself on a regular basis. They were not having any of that, so they put me in a straightjacket to keep their property from damaging itself. I did not like being in that, so again I gave up and let them do to me what they wanted to do.

One night after sleeping with twelve men, I fell into bed. I was bleeding from every place you should never bleed from. I had fallen asleep and then was awakened by a loud noise and men in my room, telling me to get up and come with them. I was scared and told them no. The one with the face mask on told me that they were there to help me. I finally believed them, got up, and ran with them to safety.

I lived this life of misery for five years, from the ages of thirteen to eighteen. No one should ever have to go through what I went through.

I will never have children because of what they did to me. I am alive and on the mend. I have to go through intense therapy every day, and one day I hope to be able to go one night without waking up in fear that someone is going to take me again.

One Spark has been a blessing to me and many other girls who have been rescued through safe homes and life skills training. I have had to retrain my mind to understand that I am worth something and deserve to be happy.

One Spark's S.T.O.P. program is nothing short of a miracle for the girls and boys that get rescued. They are the life line that keeps me going, and they have given me the will to help as many children make it back from the pit of heartache and misery they were sold into.

What would you be willing to do if I was your child? Would you be willing to give a dollar or maybe two? Would you be willing to give ten dollars or even twenty? I am asking you to help me help One Spark continue with the ministry they are providing.

They have no paid employees, and that means 100 percent of what you give goes to the cause of helping to locate, rescue, and rehabilitate these children who have been taken or who make a poor choice and wind up in a nightmare they could have never imagined.

One last thing that I want to say is this—If you do not help in this program, you have told people like me that our lives don't matter. I am sorry if you think I am being rude by saying it this way, but you never had to go through what I had to go through. I would never wish this on anyone.

You can donate on the One Spark Facebook page or at www.1Spark.net. My goal is to bring in $1,000, and that will help rescue five to ten children. Please join this awesome cause and help me do my part to help the next child who is trapped in his or her life of misery.

I want you to know that no one asked me to write this letter. I want to help, and I want to make a difference in this world.

David – Anchor or Key – God can't give bad

"There is a time for everything, and a season for every activity under the heavens." *Ecclesiastes 3:1 (NIV)*

When bad things happen in life—and I promise you, they will—you will have two choices in life: 1) use the experience as anchors and glorify the devil, or 2) use them as keys to glorify God! I know too many people for when the moment something bad happens, they seem to be stuck in time. They seemed to be anchored down in that exact spot, unable or unwilling to move forward.

Many people have had a bad childhood, and they use it as an excuse. They were beaten, molested, abandoned, and/or abused in many other ways. They seem never to be able to move forward because of these chains and anchors holding them back. When this happens, they never have the life God intended them to have—because of the inability to move forward and because of the anchor holding them in place.

My life as a child was really awful, at best. I was beaten on a regular basis, molested too many times to talk about, abandoned, and left to fend for myself.

At first, I had an anchor that would not allow me to move forward. But, one day, I woke up and realized that I could unhook the anchor that was destroying my life. I also realized that if I did not unhook that anchor, I would always be allowing the devil to rule my life with hate, anger, and distrust. I knew that if I could unhook the anchor of molestation, abandonment, and child abuse, I could one day use these situations to glorify God.

I woke up one day and unhooked my life from the anchors that were holding me in the past. I decided to use what the devil brought up every day—to tell me that I was worthless—to help others.

You see, God can't and won't ever give us bad, so when we realize that this did not come from God, we can harness the strength through him to unhook that chains that bind us and forge those chains into keys. We have the power to use every bad situation that has ever happened to us as a key. "How?" you ask. We do this by telling our stories to other people who are going through the same things that we went through in our lives.

When we choose to use our keys to unlock someone else's prison doors, it starts the healing process in our own lives. I speak to thousands of children each year, and every time I tell my story, I get to use at least one of my keys to unlock someone else's prison door and start them on the road to healing.

In my lifetime I have taken the chains of every bad situation and forged them into keys, and today I have many key on my chain that I can use to unlock many prison doors.

I hope, today, as you rise and wipe the sleep from your eyes, you will unhook anchors that are holding you back and holding you down and forge them into keys that will allow you to unlock other's prison doors.

Please share this with everyone you can, and let's see how many anchors we can unhook today!

REMEMBER THAT GOD WILL USE YOUR PAIN FOR SOMEONE ELSE'S GAIN

Married Five Times – Sparking Changed Everything

"The fact is, you have had five husbands, and the man you now have is not your husband. What you have just said is quite true." John 4:18 (NIV)

I have been on your page for six years and have been moved many times to tears. But soon after the tears, I found myself being the same nasty person I was before.

I have had a lot of success in business but no success in marriage, friendships, or other relationships. I have been married five times and each time cost me a lot of money. I cared more about the money than I did the person I was married to.

I was not raised this way. I grew up with two very loving parents who both would give the shirts off their backs to help someone else. I promised myself that I would never be poor like them. Right after college, I started a company that I still own today. It has done well, in spite of me and my nasty ways.

One day, when I was at a low point in my life and wanted to change, I found myself back on this page, reading the nice things people have done. I decided to go out and do something kind. I went out, and it did not take very long to find someone to help. There was a lady trying to get gas where I worked, and she did not have any money. I stepped up and put my credit card in and told her to fill her car up. She was so excited that she could hardly hold back the tears. I told her why I was doing the Spark and she just smiled.

I began to do this on a regular basis, and I found that people started to talk to me. I also realized that my relationships with the people who worked for me were getting better.

I asked my employees if they would like to go out and get their Spark on. I know many of them had no clue what this was all about, but they went anyway. We had a great time and continue to do this once a month.

I met a lady while I was Sparking. We fell in love with Sparking and fell in love with each other. In twenty-eight years of owning my company, I had never given a bonus to anyone, until I found One Spark.

I am getting married in a few months, and David has agreed to officiate our wedding. I called and asked if he was an ordained minister, and he said yes. I know that this marriage will be my last because I am a changed man who is all about Sparking.

EIGHTEEN, BUT MORE LIKE 135 – SEX SLAVE

"For where you have envy and selfish ambition, there you will find disorder and every evil practice." James 3:16 (NIV)

I am eighteen years old in birth years, but I am 135 years old in street years. I was very rebellious as a young girl, and that is what led my life to the pit of misery and made me try to commit suicide thirteen times.

I was thirteen when I thought I knew it all and that my parents were trying to keep me from having fun. I would sneak out and meet up with boys—yes, this was at thirteen. One bad decision led to another and soon I was living on the streets, hooked on meth. Soon I found myself being bought and sold like a piece of meat. Men would do things to me that you could never imagine.

It seemed like it was getting worse and worse. These men were doctors, lawyers, and businessmen who had a dark side to them.

I was seventeen and had made my mind up that I was going to end my life that night. I had planned it all out in my head and rehearsed it over and over again—how I was finally going to be free and never have any more pain. Well, there was one thing I never could have planned, and that was a group of people coming to the rescue.

It was about midnight and the house was quiet. Then, all of a sudden, we heard a loud noise and soon there were masked men telling us to get up and follow them. One man, who I will not name, told me that everything was going to be all right. I asked him if he promised and he told me yes.

After getting out of the house, we all piled into a van, smashed in like a herd of cattle. We went to a place where we got into another van and drove for a while.

I have felt like killing myself since the day I was rescued. Then, one day, a man who I have gotten to know, called me on the phone and told me that I would use this heartache as a key or an anchor. I told him that it was easy for him to say, because he had never been through what I had been through. He said that I was right, but that I had never been through what he experienced either. He told me of how his mother sold him to men, for money. He told me that it happened over 700 times. He then said that if he would have never pulled up his anchor, and started to use his keys that his heartaches blessed him with, he would not be there to help me move forward.

Many of you have had an opportunity to donate to the S.T.O.P. program's bus project but maybe have not been moved to do so yet. I hope that my words will move you to reach deep into your bank account to help this group continue their mission.

Your donation will help children—like me—get out of the prison they are living in.

Lots of love to everyone involved with One Spark.

THE ANGEL, CHILD WITH CANCER – PARENT PRAYS WITH ANGEL

"Do not forget to show hospitality to strangers, for by doing so some people have shown hospitality to angels without knowing it." Hebrews 13:2 (NIV)

I want to first tell you that you have motivated my family to become Spark Givers. We were like a lot of families in America—we had good jobs, nice homes, good cars, and even money left over at the end of the month. The one thing we never really thought about was the other person, until my daughter got sick with cancer.

She was stage four, nothing was working, and it looked like we would lose her. I went down to the chapel and said a prayer. When I looked up, I saw an older lady praying. When she got up, she smiled and asked me how I was doing. I replied that I was terrible and was about to lose my daughter. She gave me a hug and asked if she could come to her room and pray for her. I said yes.

We went to the room and she prayed for what seemed to be a long time. Then she got up and said, "Do not worry, your daughter will not die." She told me that we needed to get our house in order and give the glory to God. We also needed to practice being kind to others, because it showed them the love of God. She then said she needed to go, and we have never seen her since that day.

I looked up any and everything about kindness and found the One Spark Foundation and all the great things you were doing for others. I called and spoke to someone in the office and he told me to go out and do some Sparks. He told me to check out the beginning story, and he asked for our address so he could send us a box of love.

The package I received in the mail had a shirt for my daughter, bracelets, One Spark cards, and a note with instructions on what we should do as a family. I read the note to the entire family, including my daughter who was sick. She told me that she loved the idea and wanted to help. I asked the doctors if it was wise to have her help, and they said it could not do any harm.

I continued to think about the old lady who prayed for my daughter and told us that she would live and not die. I wanted to believe her words, but for some reason the only thing I could think about was losing my daughter to cancer.

We went out and did our first Spark. We bought lunch for a family who also had a child fighting cancer. We had gotten to know them over that last few years, and it seemed as if God was going to take both of our children. Their son Trent had taken a turn for the worse, was in critical condition, and was not expected to make it through the night. Our family went to his room, prayed with his parents, and then spoke directly to Trent. He asked me craziest question. "Did the angel visit you and tell you that your daughter was going to be all right?" I looked at him in shock and asked what he meant. He described the old woman who came to pray for our daughter. I was floored and stunned. I had not been to church since my daughter got sick, and I blamed God.

Well, I have been very long-winded, so I will cut right to the point here. My daughter made a full recovery and now is nine years cancer free. She just graduated from medical school and is devoting her life to helping children.

We have continued to do Sparks every day; our family is much closer because of it. We go to the children's hospital every week and give the kids a Spark. I am not sure it is supposed to be this way, but I feel like we are more blessed than the people who receive the Spark.

Thank you for what you do, and I want to let everyone know that your Spark could be the Spark that changes someone's world.

MY MOTHER DID NOTHING

"They sacrificed their sons and daughters in the fire. They practiced divination and sought omens and sold themselves to do evil in the eyes of the Lord, arousing his anger." 2 Kings 17:17 (NIV)

Hi Dave and everyone at the One Spark Foundation.

I want to first start off by telling you a little bit of my story. I was living in a violent home where my mother and her boyfriend fought every day. He was very mean and would say things to me that made me scared.

When my mom went to work, he would play touchy feely. This game was like chicken, but it involved a lot of touching. When this started I was thirteen; I did not want to make him mad. Well, touching soon led to sex and then it became very violent. He then would call his friends over and make money off of me. When my mom found out, she said, "Now you that you are a woman, you can help pay the bills." This went on for over two years.

Her boyfriend kept me there by telling me that if I left, my little sister would have to take my place. I was out one day in the park, and I started to talk to a girl about what was going on in my life. She told me that I needed to call this number and tell them what was going on. I did and I spoke to a lady that asked me a lot of questions. Then she asked me if I wanted to get out of the misery I was in, and I told her yes. She told me that she would get back to me. I got a call back a few days later and was told that there would be some men that would come and get me and my sister and take us some place safe.

The night it happened there was a knock at the door, and all of a sudden someone had me and my sister—and out the door we went. I talked to a policewoman for a while, and then I had to go to the hospital to be checked out. They found that I was infected with AIDS and had four other STDs as well.

I thought my life was over, but I have a new life caring for my little sister. I am doing much better but wake up every day with the fear of dying and leaving my little sister to someone else to raise. She is fourteen and is doing very well for what she has been through. I want her to have a safe life from predators who seek out young girls and boys to make money off of.

I guess the hardest thing for me is the fact that my mother knew what was going on but chose to do nothing about it.

Here is my plea. Please give to the One Spark Foundation that has given so much to me and my little sister. When you click 'like,' it does not have the power to change a life, but when you give, you show your true love for kids like me.

The One Spark Foundation has made sure we have the things we need, and they continue to give more than we ask for and continue to provide counseling for me and my sister.

I know that I am not a girl who was taken and sold, but I still lived a life of heartache and would still be living that misery if it was not for the One Spark team.

Every ten dollars allows them to do a search for children, and every one hundred dollars could help them rescue someone like me.

I hope that you will share this, and I hope that you will reach into your wallets and give from your hearts.

OLDEST SPARKERS MARRIED THREE SISTERS – THE JOHNSON BOYS

"A friend loves at all times, and a brother is born for adversity."
Proverbs 17:17 (NIV)

Hi, One Spark.

We are the Johnson boys and we are eighty-two, eighty-one, and eighty years young. My name is John and I am the oldest, my brother Peter is next oldest, and Paul is the baby.

I was married fifty-nine years, Peter was married fifty-four years, and Paul was married fifty-three years. We married sisters, and *wow* they were the prettiest girls in town. Of course, I married the prettiest one because I got the first pick.

The ladies we married were great women who loved God and loved doing things for other people. Our gals were great mothers, and even better grandmothers. They did all the school stuff with the kids and grandkids, and the men held down the fort at our car dealership.

We had twelve kids amongst the three families, and they in turn gave us forty-one grandbabies and seventeen great grandchildren. We loved them all. It seemed as the family grew, so did the number of car dealerships.

How we got introduced to the One Spark was when their group came to our grandchildren's school. Our wives told us boys that we had to go and listen and support the kids.

I was not excited to hear a snake oil salesman, but I knew I had to go or I'd be in big trouble with my wife. Don't you agree, men, that it's odd how we want to grow up and get married and be an adult, only to have our women tell us what to do? I loved it.

I left that school that day (at the age of seventy-one), knowing this was something our families could do—you know—the Spark thing. The women took after this like coon dogs to a coon's trail. They began to bake and we started doing Sparks for our customers. We continued to do more and more Sparks, and soon we were like the godfathers of the Sparks. Those were the happiest days of our lives.

One day my brother called and said his wife had cancer and it did not look good. The fight was on, and in the middle of his wife's battle, my wife got lung cancer. Yes, we smoked, and you should not. My wife died first, then his wife died, and then our other brother's wife got the same darn cancer. She died six months after being diagnosed.

One day after my brother's wife died, I called a meeting for the boys and told them that we were going to honor our girls with a lot of Sparks.

We all took the cars of our beautiful ladies and gave them to families that really needed them. The only thing we told the families was that they could not go telling everyone about what we did. Our children run the dealerships now, but the old men still have a say if we want it. We told our children that we wanted to pick three kids a year and give each one a scholarship to honor each one of our wives. They loved it.

We go around Sparking where we can, and this Sparking thing has definitely brought our entire family together. We sure laugh a lot because we are the oldest flame throwers in the country. We have been in contact with the One Spark people. Dave, you are a man who has blessed me. I am sorry for the mess you went through as a child. But like you say, the bad things in life are just keys waiting to be used to open up someone's prison door.

One Spark needs a mascot, a super hero of some kind like the green hornet. Boy, we used to listen to that show on the radio and loved it.

We make a day out of Sparking, and we have sure Sparked a lot of people. What we find, though, is that each time we Spark, we are the ones that get the most from the Spark.

Well, your One Spark superheroes are signing off, but rest assured we are doing our Sparks to help change the world.

Four Kids Die and Parents Had to Fight the State

"Like a club or a sword or a sharp arrow is one who gives false testimony against a neighbor." Proverbs 25:18 (NIV)

I am a mother of four, and over the years I would say that my husband and I have faced our share of heartaches. We lost our oldest child thirteen years ago in a car accident. Three years later we lost our youngest child when she fell off the swing. We were investigated and they found we did nothing wrong. Two years later we lost our second to the oldest child to heart problems. That is when child protective services opened another investigation on us. It was not bad enough to have lost our third child, but to be accused of doing something to a child that we loved more than life itself was overwhelming.

During this time, we had very little money and could not afford an attorney to defend ourselves against the state's accusations. My husband does a lot of odd jobs to help with the bills. He received a call from a man who knew someone he did work for, and he wanted my husband to come look at his air conditioning unit because he was told he needed a new one. My husband went over and looked at it. When he was finished, he told the man that his AC was fixed and he only owed him $157. He was there for over two hours and the bill included the parts. He told the man that many people in the AC business want to rip you off, but my husband told him that he was not like that.

My husband told him that he worked for a plumbing company, but he had a master's license in HVAC, plumbing, and electrical. The man asked my husband why he did not own his own business. My husband told him that he did not have the money because of the state filing charges against us for child neglect. The man my husband was working for was a family law guy and asked if he could look at his case. My husband said, "Sure."

Our last child came down with cancer, and that is when the state came at us with all they had, because they said that no one loses four children. We did, and the lawyer who my husband met helped us get through the investigation and never charged us a dime.

We now use the pain of our story to help other people move through their own agony. I read the beginning story of the One Spark Foundation, and it made me realize that it could always be worse.

We hope this story helps anyone struggling with grief. We have learned through the grace of God that we will be okay and we still have a mission on this earth.

Car Man – Second Chance

"The Lord our God is merciful and forgiving, even though we have rebelled against him." Daniel 9:9 (NIV)

This is a wonderful Spark, or group of Sparks, and yes, Sparking should start at home.

Hi, One Spark.

I am so glad I found your page because it has encouraged me to do things for other people. I have lived a life all about me and not caring about anyone or anything else. That attitude landed me in prison for twelve years for selling drugs. I left behind a wife and three kids. When I got out, they did not know me and my wife had divorced me. I have been working hard at rebuilding my relationship with my family. I realized that my Sparking needed to start at home.

I looked for a job for months, but I couldn't find what I wanted. So I took a job and decided that I would make the best of it. I started cleaning cars, then moved to detailing them, and then into sales. As a salesman, I found my calling. I told myself that I would always put the customers' needs first, no matter what. This almost cost me my job a couple of times because I told them to buy from a different lot, because what we had would not solve their needs. The owner of the company soon realized that I could be trusted to make decisions, because of the decisions that I made to serve our customers. I moved into a small apartment that was not nice, so I could give my family all the extra money I was making. The checks started out small, but soon I was giving them a lot of money a month. I made sure that my kids and ex-wife had what they needed and that my ex-wife could do for herself. I told her to stop working and care for our kids. I told her to help out at the school.

My ex-wife's car was terrible and she was in need of a new one. I asked my boss if I could find a car for her, while taking payments out of my check, and he said yes. That is when the general manager told me that I should not have approached the owner without talking to him first. I then got written up. I kept working hard for the owner, but I began to hate my job because of the general manager. I knew he was a very dishonest person, but I also knew he would never get fired because he was the owner's son-in-law.

I was doing so well that other dealers were trying to get me to come to work for them. I always told them no until I was offered an assistant general manager position with a larger dealership. I waited until our general manager left, and I went in to talk to the owner. I told him that I was going to be giving my two weeks' notice because I was offered the assistant general manager position at another dealership. He asked me if it was just the money and I told him no, the general manager was not honest and he was a jerk. I told him that we were missing money from the service side, and I was sure it was him. He said to me, "You're right! In fact, I'm firing him tomorrow and offering you the general manager position as well. I'll match his salary." I started to cry and asked him why he was so good to me. He simply answered, "Because you've been good to me." This raise allowed me to move my family into a great home, with a pool for my kids. My ex and I are now dating, and things are great. We go out as a family and do Sparks two times a week.

I have taken 5 percent of my pay and put it in an account to help our employees in their times of need. Mr. X, the owner now, matches what I give. We have started a Spark night at our dealership and go into the community and help those in need. Our dealership was never in the top, but we are now number ten in the nation. We have purchased two more dealerships in our town and have turned the culture there. We have introduced them to the Spark Giver's mindset. Some of the old employees never wanted to change, so we made a change of personnel, and we have grown so fast. I am getting married soon, and Dave is going to be the minister. If you don't like the life you have, you and you alone can change it. It starts with an attitude of gratitude and a heart of giving.

We are asked how our dealerships do so well, and I always say that we are selling love and kindness, with the focus on putting the customers' needs first.

Thank you for the guiding light that has been put up for the world to follow.

LADY LOST HUSBAND AND KIDS

"He will wipe every tear from their eyes. There will be no more death or mourning or crying or pain, for the older order of things has passed away." Revelation 21:4 (NIV)

Today was not a good day for me. Our daughter just lost her long fight with cancer, and I was mad, hurt, and thought that life couldn't possibly get any worse for me and my family. That thought process all changed when a nurse told me that a family of eight was in a terrible auto accident and it did not look good.

I was in the waiting room, waiting on our family to come, so we could head home. That is when a mother came rushing in. She was frantic and wanted answers to her questions. They had no answers for her at the moment. I looked around and saw that she was all alone, so I walked over and asked her if I could help her with anything. That is when she snapped and said that her family was involved in a horrible accident. I told her about our family losing our daughter that day and we sat and started to talk.

I told my family to go on home and that I would be there soon. This was at 3 PM. Before I knew it, it was 9 PM and my husband was calling me, asking me what was going on and if I needed him to came back to the hospital. I told him that I was okay and would be staying with Karen until her family could get there from Canada.

The next fifteen hours were the worst fifteen hours of my life; they were worse than the last fifteen hours of my daughter's life. Karen's husband and seven of her children were in this accident. Over the next fifteen hours, she lost her husband and three of her children. The next four days were no better to her, because two more of her children passed away.

I stayed with her and did not leave the hospital for two days. Her family started to arrive, and I told her that I would give them time together and that I would go home. I continued to visit the hospital for the next two months until all of her children were home. I have been helping her for the last four months with her children and household matters.

I hope that we all realize that no matter what we are going through, there is always someone who has it worse than we do. I still have a lot of pain because of the loss of my daughter, who loved One Spark, but helping someone else has made the pain much less than what it would have been. My friend lost five of her children and her husband in that terrible accident, but their lives gave life to many other people.

I am not sure if you would count this as a Spark, but it sure feels like one.

EIGHTY-NINE-YEAR-OLD GRANNY – VET WITH ONE ARM AND LEG

"And we urge you, brothers and sisters, warn those who are idle and disruptive, encourage the disheartened, help the weak, be patient with everyone." 1 Thessalonians 5:14

I am on social security and have very little money. I found myself complaining about what I did not have and believing other people had more than I did. One day I was going to get my food from the store, and I met a man who was in the war and is now homeless. He lost an arm and leg, and he was a happy man. I asked him why he was so happy, as he had lost so much. He told me that he had not lost that much because there were people who lost their lives. He told me that so many people get caught up in complaining about what they do not have that they forget to see what they have been blessed with, and forget to give thanks.

I asked him if he was hungry and he said yes. We went into the store and bought him some food and a few other things he needed. I sat outside and talked with him for hours. When it was time to go, he thanked me for all that I did for him. I said, "Thank you for opening my eyes to all the blessings I have been given." I then gave him my last twenty dollars. For the first time in a long time, I was not worried about where I was going to get this or that for anything.

I am a blessed person who now can see what is really important. You see, it was not the Spark I gave this man that really is the big thing here. It is the Spark he gave me that has forever changed my life.

For anyone who reads my words, stop complaining and start counting your blessings. Don't tell this old woman you have nothing to be thankful about, because I will have to find you and swat your bottom. I am eighty-nine years old and feel like I am thirty again. I wake up happy and loving life. It does not matter what you have; the only thing that matters is if you give thanks for what you have been blessed with in life.

Love, Granny and happy as a lark.

MILDRED AND KIM TO HARVARD

"All day long he craves and craves, but the righteous gives and does not hold back." Proverbs 21:26 (ESV)

I live in a very poor area of town and often worry about my children's safety. I have been blessed to have a good job, cleaning for a lady (Mildred) who is very nice. She loves my children and treats them as if they were her very own.

I have three kids: ages of nine, sixteen, and seventeen. The seventeen-year-old is graduating from high school, has made great grades, and has always wanted to attend Harvard. We have known that this might not be possible, unless she got a lot of scholarships, and even then we might still not be able to afford it.

Kim took her ACT tests and only missed one question, which is amazing from what her teachers told me. I never graduated high school because I got pregnant and had to go to work to support my child. I got married and had the best life until my husband got cancer and died.

Kim was sending her applications to a lot of schools and many sent back acceptance letters. Kim would talk to Mildred about the school stuff and she knew how to write up those applications to help my baby get into school. Mildred told Kim that she knew she would get into Harvard and she would do well there. Mildred was very rich and knew a lot of people who could help Kim with her dreams. Mildred made several calls to many people and asked for help, and soon Harvard sent a letter telling my baby she was in. I was shocked and now had to figure out how to pay for the school bills. Mildred called me into her office and asked, "How long have you worked for me?" I said, "Fourteen years." She asked me how many times she had given me a bonus, and I told her, "Never." She looked at me and said that she had been investing my bonuses. Kim had enough money to attend Harvard, and I would not have to worry about a thing. I stood there and started to cry, and she came over and gave me a great big hug and told me she loved me.

I have to admit that I knew she cared for me, but I always saw myself just as a black woman and nothing more. She told me that I needed to look in the mirror and see what she has seen for those fourteen years—a beautiful lady, with a heart of gold.

Mildred explained that Kim could receive her gift—under one condition. I said, "What's that?" Mildred then told me about the One Spark page. "Tell Kim that she must complete one hundred Sparks before I give her the money," she said. She requested a meeting with Kim, and I told her that I would set it up.

Kim went to see Mildred, and that's when Mildred told her that she was going to pay for her college. Mildred instructed her to visit the One Spark site and read all she could about it. She added that Kim needed to do one hundred Sparks. Mildred gave Kim the funds to complete the Sparks; however, she told her that for 50 percent of them, she could not use any money at all.

This task changed my daughter forever. Mildred asked Kim to write down the Sparks she completed and then hand the notes over to her. I was there when Mildred read what my daughter did, and I saw her start to cry after she read the first one. Mildred read them out loud to me and I was crying because of the beauty of her Sparks. Kim is loving school, and now my other two kids and I have moved in with Mildred. We do Sparks each day as a family, and I have never been happier. Nor has Mildred.

Thank you, One Spark, for teaching us the power of loving someone else.

Bethany Garage Sale at High School $72,136

"The father of a righteous child has great joy; a man who fathers a wise son rejoices in him. May your father and mother rejoice; may she who gave you birth be joyful." Proverbs 23:24–25 (NIV)

My daughter, Bethany, is fourteen and loves her stuff, like most kids her age. She has three younger brothers who are always testing her love when they get into her things.

She came home one day and asked if she could sell all of her belongings to help give toys to the kids who are sick in the hospital. I asked her why she would want to do this, and she looked me in the eyes and said, "Because it is the right thing to do; it is just stuff."

My husband and I are both doctors and have always spoiled our kids to the point that we ask each of them, "Do you think you will ever want to leave our house?" I asked Bethany if she was sure that this is what she wanted to do, and she said yes.

The next day she was in her room making flyers for my husband and me to give to everyone at the hospital. I was making my rounds and giving out the flyers, when one of the nurses told me that she was going to have a garage sale, but she wanted to donate all of her things to the 'Toys for Smiles' sale. I had several people tell me that they would donate, and then I became nervous about where we would put everything being contributed.

I called my daughter and explained that we were going to have to find a new place to have the sale, and she told me that the high school said she could have it there in the parking lot.

Bethany rallied several of her classmates to help organize the sale. The school was receiving calls about where and when people could donate their items. Many people were getting involved, and pretty soon this sale had taken on a life of its own. It was on the news, and more people wanted to help and give.

Bethany raised $72,136 from the garage sale, and she sold most of what she had to give. As parents, this was a very happy moment for us because we had felt that we had spoiled our kids to the point that they would never want to give back to the world—Boy, were we ever wrong!

To everyone who helped Bethany organize this big sale, I want to say thank you. To all that donated, I want to say thank you, thank you, and thank you for your help. None of this would have been possible without you.

Love, a very proud mom.

HOMELESS MAN OFF OF THE STREETS – GIVES BACK

"Now He who supplies seed to the sower and bread for food will supply and multiply your seed for sowing and increase the harvest of your righteousness." 2 Corinthians 9:10 (ESV)

I wanted to thank you for helping me when I was homeless. You fed me and loved me until I had the courage to get back on my feet and off drugs. Many people and groups had tried to help me, but I refused. Then you came along with your crazy leader who loved me right off the bat. I have never had a man walk up to me and tell me he loved me before. I have to admit that I thought he was hitting on me at first, and then some of the women who helped with One Spark told me that he did love me and was not hitting on me.

I can remember times when I would get thirty or forty hugs to get my food, and WOW it is great food. I did not like the hugs at first; I just got them to eat the wonderful food. I can tell you that no one in town feeds food that good. I asked the crazy leader hug guy, "Why do you give us such great food?" He answered, "Because that is what Jesus wants me to do." I told him that he would be better to offer food like everyone else and feed more people, and he said, "No, it would not." He was kind of firm about it, and then he said to me, "If you were going to feed Jesus, would you feed him ordinary food?" I said, "No." He went on to say that he loved all of us and would never do that, because when you feed the best to those you love, they can taste your love in the food.

One Spark works with a church that brings clothes for us. One day Dave walked over and asked me if I needed prayer, and then he took me over to the church group and they prayed for me. Another time, Dave, the crazy leader who loves everyone, came over to me and told me that it was time that I got off the streets and got my life straight. Then another woman came over and asked me if I needed help getting into treatment. She did help me, and I now have been clean for over two years.

One Spark helped me find an apartment. They gave me furniture and appliances that were donated to them—they did not charge me a dime! I know that you guys love me and love everyone you help. My life has changed so much because I have an apartment and now have a relationship with my kids and family again.

To all at One Spark and to all who help with your support, I want you to know that I am a life that has been saved—because if I never got off the streets, I would be dead. One Spark, I know it is not a lot, but here is twenty-five dollars from my paycheck. I have had a good job for one and a half years now, and I want to help the next person. I really want to thank the One Spark lady who drove me to get help and who came to see me every day. Thank you for the books and the Bible.

RACISM ENDS WITH LOVE (LAWYER)

"So God created mankind in his own image, in the image of God he created them; male and female he created them." Genesis 1:27 (ESV)

Hi everyone.

I want to tell you about a Spark that was given to my husband and me over thirty years ago. My husband is an attorney and, at the time, he was representing a man who was linked to the Ku Klux Klan (KKK). My husband was on a rotation to be called when people couldn't afford an attorney.

He took the case, and many people were very upset with us because he did so. In fact, several people threatened my husband. We lived several towns away, and the town that the case was in was mainly a black community.

My husband was leaving one night when several men confronted him about working for a KKK member. I truly believe that if a few other black men would not have stopped them, he would have been hurt.

The fellow who helped my husband asked why he would represent such a scumbag. He said, "Everyone—no matter how bad of a person they are—deserves legal representation." The young men understood.

About five years later, one of the young men was accused of raping a white girl. He didn't have the money to obtain the services of a good lawyer. The mama of the young man called my husband and asked for assistance, and he said to her, "I would love to help." She offered him her savings of $1,000 to pay for his services. He replied, "I appreciate your gesture, and thank you for offering; however, your son did not ask for money from me when he helped me years ago."

My husband was sixty-four years old at the time and had retired from the law firm he started and then later sold. We had been blessed very well in life and had no children to leave anything to, so he thought, *What better way to give back than to help people in trouble who need a lawyer?!*

My husband represented this man and he was, eventually, found not guilty. They became very close and the young man went on to become a lawyer himself. You see, we make too much fuss about racial issues, instead of making a promise to our hearts that we will never treat another person differently because of the color of their skin.

My husband passed away two months ago, and he had a wonderful funeral. There were many in attendance: lawyers, police officers, and a lot of people who my husband helped in tough situations. The young man who first aided my husband (who then later my husband helped), was the main speaker at his funeral. He told of the love my husband had for him and the love that he had for both of us. He went on to say that many of his friends had called him an Uncle Tom, because he had become so close to a white man. He described the businessmen who said things to my husband about having him as a friend. He relayed the story of the time my husband told a partner in business that he could no longer be partners because of the comments he was making about his friend who happened to be black.

This man told the many people who attended the funeral that the only thing that was going to stop racism was love. He stressed to everyone that both sides needed to stop spreading hate, and start walking in love instead.

The last thing he told everyone was that when we came to see him at school, many people asked them if we were his parents, and he said yes. He went on to tell everyone that he got to attend Harvard because of us, and that is when I stood up and told everyone there that he got to attend Harvard because he worked hard.

I am now ninety-three years old and feel that I have been blessed more than I should have been blessed. I had the best husband for seventy-five years, and God blessed me with a son, a daughter, and two grandchildren.

No matter what anyone tells you, you can love one another. Please make a promise that you will love everyone you meet. I hope that this is a Spark.

Dear Mr. Hill, I love what you have and are doing with this group. Keep up the great work.

HAND UP NOT OUT

"For even when we were with you, we gave you this rule: 'If a man will not work, he shall not eat.'" 2 Thessalonians 3:10 (NIV)

I was homeless for many years, until One Spark helped me get back on my feet. They helped me understand that if I wanted a different life, I was going to have to make some different choices. They taught me life skills so I could go out in the world and get a job. I worked in their job training program that is kind of like college but you don't have to pay for it; they pay you.

Once I got through my life skills and on-the-job training classes, they found me a good job in a hotel. I have been on my own, off the streets, and free of drugs for over two years now. I thought that they were being mean when they told me that I needed to better myself and get off the streets. They told me that if I was willing to work hard, they would help me, and they did for sure.

If it was not for the big Spark you gave me I would still be on the streets doing drugs and being a messed up person. Thank you, and because of your help, I now have my kids living with me. They are happy and liking the house we live in.

Thanks, from homeless no more.

LOVE WHAT MATTERS

"And now these three remain: faith, hope, and love. But the greatest of these is love." 1 Corinthians 13:13 (NIV)

This evening, as I was leaving Best Buy, I noticed this man going through the garbage can outside of the store. As I walked to my car, I watched him as he reached into the garbage can to pull out fast food trash bags, inspecting each one. He did this for several minutes. He would find a few fries in one bag and a bite or two of a hamburger in another bag. I could see the hamburger wrapper by his knee where he was placing the food items he'd found.

He never bothered anyone or tried to stop and beg for money as people entered and left the store. After he went through the entire trash can, he neatly cleaned up the area and wrapped up the food he found in the dirty hamburger wrapper. My heart literally hurt for him. I am not someone who just hands out money or even helps homeless people because so many are not truly homeless. I don't believe I've ever seen someone actually go through a garbage can to try to find food to eat.

I knew I had to help him. I got out of my car and asked him if I could buy him something to eat. He told me he would appreciate anything I could get him. He was on a bike and I told him if he'd follow me, I'd buy him a meal at the fast food place around the block. He followed me and I bought him the biggest meal they had on the menu. The only request he gave me for his order was if I could get him a big glass of sweet tea to go with his meal! When I brought him his food, he was so thankful. He told me his name was Steve and he'd been homeless ever since his sister died last September. He was trying to get off the streets, but it was so hard. I told him God loved him and I would pray for him. He told me again how much he appreciated the meal.

When I got back in my car, I drove off with such a heaviness in my heart for this man. I drove down the road and felt compelled to go back to help him. When I came back he had finished his meal and was riding away. I pulled up beside him and asked him if there was any way I could help him. He said, "Not really." He never asked me for money. I asked, "Can I buy you a few meals and put them on a gift card for you?" He answered, "That would be so kind." I drove to McDonald's, bought him some meals, and gave him a gift card.

He broke down crying. He told me that he prayed for me today! I wasn't sure what he meant (I was assuming he was praying for me for what I did for him), so I thanked him. He said, "No, you don't understand. I prayed that God would send someone to buy me a hot meal today...and he sent you!" I didn't know what to say—I was speechless! Praying for a hot meal wasn't a prayer I had prayed today! Come to think of it, that's not a prayer I've ever prayed! I always pray over my food, but I've never prayed for a meal; it's expected! I've never doubted that I wouldn't be able to eat. Tears began to fill my eyes! Oh my, how blessed am I. Maybe God used me to answer this man's prayer—to let him know that He cares for Him and knows what he is going through! But, maybe God used this man to show me just how blessed I am and what I take for granted.

He said, "You see, I have cancer!" He pulled up his shirt and pointed to a huge mass that was poking out from his stomach. He said he knew it wouldn't be much longer. I asked him if he knew Jesus. He told me that he did. I asked if I could pray for him and he said that I could. We prayed right there on the sidewalk of McDonald's. Tears poured from his eyes. He told me he knew that he was going to die and that he was ready to do so. He was tired of being in pain and felt he would be better off dead because there was no life living that way. I stayed and encouraged him for a few minutes, trying to fight back my tears. My prayer is that I showed him the love of Jesus today—that something I said gave him hope.

You see, everybody has a story! I know Steve's story now—all because I felt compelled to help him—he ended up touching me today!

When I left him, I knew I had done what God wanted me to do! God put him in my path today. I know He did! I've never sensed such a feeling before in helping someone as I did today. I was reminded again of how blessed I am! I have a vehicle that takes me from place to place. I have a roof over my head, clean clothes, and money to buy hot meals, running water, electricity, my health, a job, family, and friends! Sometimes God sends situations our way to remind us of how blessed we are. If you've read this far, please remember Steve in your prayers!

Yes, I have been blessed; God is so good to me. Precious are His thoughts of you and me! There's no way I could count them. There's not enough time, so I'll just thank Him for being so kind. God has been good, so good! I have been blessed!

Anchor to Key – Her Story Changed a School

"And the angel said to her, 'Do not be afraid, Mary, for you have found favor with God.'" Luke 1:30 (NIV)

I am from a high school you spoke at many years ago, and it touched me so much. I have not had a great childhood; it is similar to yours in many ways. I have never thought of using what has happened to me in the past as a key. I have gone through my life using everything bad that has ever happened to me as an anchor. I have used them as excuses to not move forward and to make poor decisions in my life.

The day after you left our school, I sat down and had a come-to-Jesus meeting with myself. I did not like it, but it needed to be done. I had to tell myself to stop anchoring down from a bad situation and to start to manufacture keys that will unlock people's prison doors.

I never thought that my story could help anyone, but I have to tell you that I have started to share it with all who will listen, and I have had several people tell me that my story has given them hope—and that they will to continue to fight.

I have to tell several young girls that NO still means NO, and that they did nothing wrong. We live in a town where football is everything, and girls have been just objects for the boys' pleasure. Well, the tide is changing in my little town. It all started with one voice, or one key, being put into another person's heart. Soon there were several ex-prisoners, standing in a circle, who took a pledge not to let this happen anymore. There were girls, boys, athletes, honor students, and many adults. Our town was in the paper for a long time, and I do not want to open up old wounds. I wanted to tell you that One Spark can change the world, and I am proof of that, because it changed our small town.

Here is my plea to every person who reads these words. Never stop believing that your Spark can change the world. Your Spark may be your voice, and I know firsthand that a voice can be a great Spark

ONE SPARK IN AFRICA – SANDWICH WAS THE KEY

"If your enemy is hungry, give him food to eat; if he is thirsty, give him water to drink." Proverbs 25:21 (NIV)

I live in Africa and have very little money because of the economic struggles here in this country. I am thankful to be employed where I am. I work several odd jobs to care for my family.

One day I was on the bus and a man from Ghana asked me if I would like a sandwich, because he had two. I said, "Thank you, yes." He gave me the sandwich and a One Spark Foundation card. I read it and then asked what it was all about. He said, "You need to spread love to everyone you meet!" I ate the sandwich and then told him, "This is not possible because there are so many bad people in this world we live in." He replied, "Well, we must be kind even when they are mean."

The following day I was on my way to work, and a few policemen started to harass me. I wanted to fight back, but I relayed to them the message the man on the bus had given me yesterday. I told the policemen that I loved them and that it was okay to pick on me. One of them hit me and again I told him that I loved him. I had some hard candy and asked him if he would like a piece of it—or he could have it all. That is when one of the other policemen told him to stop. He asked me why I was so nice, and I gave him the One Spark Foundation card I was given. I said, "This is why." The policeman promised to look it up online.

I was on my way home from work when the nice policeman asked me to get in his car. I was a little scared, but I went anyway. He told me that he was going to give me a ride home. When we got to my house, he asked if he could come inside and I said yes. We do not have many things in our home because we can't afford them. The policeman looked all around and then said he had to leave. A few hours later he returned with several people. They gave us two beds, a couch, a chair, and a few other things. He handed me back the One Spark Foundation card and told me he loved me. I was in shock and so was my family. We hugged and they left. I told my wife of the things that happened and she said it was God working through the One Spark Foundation card.

I practice Sparks all the time and love what you are about. I have handmade many cards to give when I am Sparking. This is most rewarding.

STORY KEY – YOUNG MAN FROM GAY TO MARRIED

"A new command I give you: Love one another. As I have loved you, so you must love one another." John 13:34 (NIV)

I am a seventeen-year-old male and I am gay. I go to a small-town school and it has been hard to want to go to school because people make fun of me and call me names. Over the years I have tried to commit suicide several times, but someone came to my rescue each time.

Our school was having a guy come speak about being kind and the power of positive choices. I found out the name of the group and looked them up. When I did, I thought I did not want to go because the man seemed to speak of God a lot, and every Christian I had ever dealt with, up to this point, only wanted to tell me that I was going to spend eternity with the devil. I made up my mind that I was not going to hear this clown tell me about how my lifestyle was wrong.

So, two days before One Spark came to speak at our school I was on their Facebook page, and I read a lot of what had been written. I thought, *I am going to go hear this nut speak.*

When Dave started to speak, I could hear the pain that he had been through in his life, and it amazed me that he could be positive.

He told of the many things he had been through and how much pain was inside of him until he learned to use his pain as a key to unlock other people's prison doors. His speech was not what I expected from a Christian; it was full of love, laughter, and kindness. He told the group that their Spark had the power to change the world, and the only unknown was if they would use it to do so.

After Dave finished his speech and everyone headed back to class, I asked my teacher if I could be late so I could speak to him. This teacher knows all that I have been through, so she said yes. I walked up and introduced myself to him and told him that I was gay, and he said right back to me, "That is nice and I am straight." I told him that I have been picked on because I am gay. He told me that he was sorry that people are mean and just stupid. This is when I told him that I knew that he was a Christian and that he did not like gay people. He said, "You're right on both points. I do not like gay people. I love them, as I try to love all people."

Dave said that I needed to rise up and not let people occupy mind space they are not paying rent on. He told me that, today, people don't like me because I am gay and tomorrow people will not like me for many other reasons besides that one. He told me that many people are insecure and that is why they make fun of people.

Dave said he had to get going, but he told me that he wanted to give me something that his father gave him. It was a silver dollar. He told me that he had given this one to a man who served in the military and then was killed overseas. The family gave the coin back to Dave and now he was giving it to me. I asked if he had a coin for himself, and he told me that he had given it to someone else. I told him to keep the one he just gave to me, and Dave said, "The coins were given to me so that I could pass them on to someone else." The coin meant that you knew someone loved you, and that you needed to love other people. I sat there and started to cry, and that is when Dave gave me a hug and told me he loved me.

This was four years ago. I am sorry I am just now writing you about how that moment in my life made such a huge impact on me. I am getting married to a young woman who is so full of love. I introduced her to the One Spark Foundation and the power to love and how that can change the world.

Dave, I want you to know that you have to post this letter because I love you for walking in love with me and for teaching me the power of kindness. You told me that you are the frog with the most warts, and my friend I want you to know that your warts are what make you so beautiful. The fact that you do not act like you have it all together—that you still fail—makes you someone I want to be like.

I want each of you on this One Spark page to know that your words of love and kindness mean so very much to so many people.

Love, happy for the first time in my life.

CAROL – HELP WAS THE KEY

"One who oppresses the poor to increase his wealth and one who gives to the rich – both come to poverty." Proverbs 22:16 (NIV)

Today I went to a little café to meet a friend for lunch, and right outside the window where I was sitting was a homeless lady who looked hungry and sad. I have never been one to really care about the homeless, because I thought it was their choice to be on the streets. I have to say that since my friend introduced me to the One Spark page, my thought process has changed a lot.

I was raised in a very wealthy home and got almost everything I wanted. I then married a man with a lot of money, or I guess his family was very rich. You see, a lot of times families with money have their kids marry into other families with money. We could get into the why, but that is another conversation to be had later.

My husband has always treated people as if they were beneath him, and many times he is very rude. I think he has lived his life to make others miserable.

I have been blessed to have the same best friend for twenty years.

She does not come from money, and she is all about treating others with love and kindness. She is the one who introduced me to the One Spark page, and she has always told me that I needed to change. Ever since we were young, she has been telling me to be nice, kind, and loving to everyone. I usually laughed and said, "Okay," and many times I went right back to being a nasty, spoiled person. She would get on me and tell me that I was going to have to change, or one day might not like my life when I was old.

When I finally started to get it, my husband would say, "Grow up and realize that we are better than those people." Dave, I know this statement makes you so mad, because they are just people who have fallen on hard times. My husband and I started to fight every day about me wanting to help those less fortunate than us. He became even a bigger jerk, and then it got to where he became violent with me. I had enough and decided to leave him, but I was very scared as to what my parents would say and how they would treat me, since it would be the first divorce in our family. I left him, and my family was very supportive; they told me that they would always love me.

Now, fast forward nineteen months later, to me at the café, waiting on my friend, Molly, to show up. I saw the homeless woman outside, and it was cold. I got up and walked outside and told her to come in and eat with me. She told me her name was Carol and declined my invitation at first, but later gave in. I think when we walked in to the café, everyone in the restaurant was staring at us. I didn't care. We sat at our table, and the waiter came over and asked if he could get her anything. She said, "Yes, something hot." We sat and talked for fifteen minutes before Molly arrived. I introduced her to Carol and they started to chat like they had known each other for years. Molly found out everything about Carol, who had just turned twenty-two the day before. My friend can be a bit loud, and when the waiter came back she told him it was Carol's birthday. We made a big deal about her birthday. I asked Carol what she wanted to do for her late birthday present, and she replied, "I'd love a bath, a haircut, and a style." Molly works for one of my father's companies, so I called him and told him what we were doing, and he said to do what we needed to do. We spent the whole day with Carol and ate dinner with her. I asked her where she was staying and she answered, "The shelter." I said, "No, we will get you a hotel room instead." Again, it was easy to do because we own several hotels where we live. We got her tucked in and we left. The next day I called our entire family together. I am the youngest of nine kids and so we have a big family. I told them about Carol and what had happened to her. They all wanted to help out, so we made a plan. Then I went to the room to get Carol, and when she came to the door, she was smiling so big, it made my heart smile. Our family bought her lots of new clothes and many other personal items. My father told her she could stay at the hotel as long as she needed to in order to get back on her feet. Carol was not on drugs; she was running from an abusive relationship.

Long story short—Carol works for our family now, and she has moved up in the business in the last twelve months. She has her own place and car. She goes out every day and tries to give back. Carol is like a member of the family and is at every function we have. She has met someone special and will surely marry before I do. Yes, I have met a wonderful man who does not come from money, but rather from a family that knows how to love.

First Tire Change – Spark Mates

"After this the Lord appointed seventy-two others and sent them two by two ahead of him to every town and place where he was about to go." *Luke 10:1 (NIV)*

I have watched this page for a while and have read everything David and everyone else has written and posted. I started out by picking up my neighbor's paper, putting a One Spark card in it, and then placing it on her porch. I then put a little treat in her paper along with another One Spark card. I then sent a few emails and notes to

111

friends. Several of them said that they were so nice that they made them cry.

I decided to move up the ladder by assisting someone whose vehicle had broken down and really needed help. I looked for an opportunity for about three weeks and never saw one person. Then my big day came. There was an older couple in their car on the side of the road. I pulled in behind them and turned on my flashers. As I was walking up to the car, I saw they had a flat. I was met with a smile from the lady behind the wheel. I told her I was there to help her change her tire and I needed her to pop the trunk. She did, but then I was clueless on what to do next. The woman at the wheel was eighty-one years old and her husband had just left the hospital after having heart surgery.

I tried to call my husband for help, but he was in a meeting. I started to ask for the manual for the car, and as I turned around, there was the lady I was trying to help. She asked me if I had ever changed a tire before and I said, "No." She said, "I will tell you how to do it."

"How do you know how to change a tire?" I inquired. The woman replied, "The farm." She told me to get the jack out of the trunk and then instructed me step by step until the flat was changed out. "This has been the best day of my life!" I was beaming. "If anyone were to come upon us right now, they would think it was the worst day of your life— the way you look!" We spoke a bit more before she said, "Hang on a minute." She then walked up to her car to search for her wallet. I told her that I did not want her money. She replied, "It is okay to want to try and help family." I said, "I don't have money issues, but I do have giving issues. I come from a very wealthy family and have also married into quite a wealthy family. She asked, "Then why are you doing this, dear?" I replied, "I have a card for you." She took it from me, read it, and started to cry. I asked her if she was all right and she told me she was crying tears of joy. "This is a really neat thing you came up with," she said. I told her that this was not my original idea. "Some guy came up with it; if you have a computer, you can read his story." I asked her where she lived. It turns out that she and her husband live only a few miles from me. We get together often, and she has become my Spark mate.

$1.25 SPARK

"And do not neglect doing good and sharing, for with such sacrifices God is pleased." Hebrews 13:16 (NIV)

All my life I have been performing Sparks in any way possible. On November 29, 2015, my husband suffered a major heart attack. While the doctors were performing triple bypass surgery, they found kidney cancer, which had already spread to his lungs (stage four). Well, long story short, he's working very hard to beat this. I have had Sparks done for me lately, and it's such a wonderful feeling knowing that there are others doing what I did and still do, in some way, shape, or form. It always comes back to you. Some people in our lives have to force us to take the Sparks. For instance, I belong to a family of three that helps others; we are not used to being on the receiving end. You just never know what someone is going through. When we do a Spark, it may be the one thing that sets a series in motion that really helps someone else.

I will explain about the Spark that really stands out for me. It happened immediately after my husband's heart surgery and cancer diagnosis. I was a complete and utter wreck. I had to get something to drink because my mouth was so dry. I really didn't feel well and wasn't even thinking straight. I made a quick stop at the McDonald's drive-thru before heading back to the hospital. I was simply told that my Coke was paid for, and I said, "Wait…what? By who?" The cashier smiled and sent me on my way, but that simple $1.25 gesture probably saved me from a nervous breakdown. I pulled my car over and cried for what seemed like an hour because someone cared enough to do that for me. I have no idea if the worker recognized my shaking, nervous hands or my words of apology for not having my purse ready, or if someone before me had paid. The main thing is that I had hope again, and, yes, I thanked God for helping me and asked Him to bless the person who cared enough. Today my husband's heart is healed and he is going through chemotherapy, but that one gesture helped me so much. Thank you for all you do, One Spark!

MYA AUSTRALIA

"Truly I tell you, anyone who will not receive the kingdom of God like a little child will never enter it." Luke 18:17 (NIV)

Today I went to the hospital to see my friend Mary, who has a child by the name of Mya who is dying of cancer. I went in to the room to say hello and then her little girl asked me for a favor. I told her I would do anything. She said, "Will you look after my mum? And will you get One Spark on the phone, so I might speak to them?" I did not know what the Spark was, but I promised that I would honor both of her requests. I told Mary that I would be right back, and then I went to the place in the hospital where you could use the computer. I looked up One Spark and started to read all about the wonderful things they were doing around the world.

Since I'm in Australia, I did not know how I would be able to get them on the phone, because of the time change. I sent them an email, and the next morning when I woke up, there was a returned message from the man himself—yeah, the founder/custodian, Mr. Hill. I told him that Mya wanted to speak to him about an idea she had, and he told me that he would call us on the phone the next morning at 9 AM.

I went back to the hospital room and told Mary and Mya the news. I asked them how they knew of this foundation in the States, and they told me that someone had sent them a post and they have been hooked ever since.

The following morning the phone rang, and the man on the other end asked for Mya. She said hello, and they talked for almost an hour. Mr. Hill spoke to her mum for a minute or two and then that was it.

I asked Mary, "What in the world did they talk about for so long?" She answered, "I will let you know soon." The following day, I went up to the hospital to see Mary and Mya. When I got there, they were busy making plans to Spark the kids in the hospital. They asked me how much I wanted to donate to the project smile campaign. I asked what it was all about, and they said they were going to do Christmas in March. They had people come to the hospital dressed as elves, whose job was to find out what each child wanted for Christmas in March. Soon we had a list, checked it one hundred times, and then it was time to put the squeeze on everyone to help out. Mr. Hill said that One Spark would match what we raised up to $3,000. We raised that amount in one day. The nurses, doctors, and everyone else at the hospital got in on the event. They wanted to make sure not to violate any child's rights.

We Sparked eighty-five kids, and it was amazing. I am such a fan of the One Spark Foundation and all that they are dong to make the world a better place. Mya's last wish was to Spark the kids in the hospital. She did not want the media involved—only people with love in their hearts. Mya passed away five days after this wonderful event. She was able to speak to her hero one more time. Dave, as he asked me to call him, spoke to Mya for over two hours. He told her that she was his hero and that he wished he could trade places with her. She said to Dave, "That is not a good idea, because God has so much left for you to do!" I know that when Mya handed the phone to her mom, Mary said to Dave, "You have no clue what you have done for my little girl." And Dave responded, "Well, you have no clue what your daughter has done for me!" I asked to speak to Dave, and when we were almost finished, the last thing Dave said to me was, "I love you, and make sure Mary and Mya know they are loved as well." I told him thank you and that I would pass on his love.

I only have one regret about the conversation I had with Dave, and that was not telling him I loved him back. Some men are so stupid about telling another man that they love him. They think that it shows they are gay—not that there is anything wrong with that—but most men want to show how tough they are and they think by saying "I love you," it makes them weak. I know that to be able to say this makes you a real man.

Dave, I LOVE YOU, AND THANK YOU FOR ALL THE LOVE YOU SHOWED MARY, MYA, AND ME.

FAMILY LOST ON SKI TRIP

"Trust in the Lord with all your heart and lean not on your own understanding, in all your ways submit to him, and he will make your paths straight." Proverbs 3:5–6 (NIV)

I have been on this One Spark page for several years and really have done nothing except to visit it to get my bucket filled. I have not been mentally able to do anything other than that, due to the fact that I lost my husband and three kids in a terrible auto accident. My children had asked their dad to take them skiing and snowboarding. My husband loved to ski, and he told me that we were going to take the whole family on a fun-filled vacation.

My husband set the date to go skiing and then told us to get ready to have a blast on the slopes. He was so excited to spend time with the family and create memories that our children would have for the rest of their lives. One week before we were to leave on our family trip, my mother fell and broke her hip. She was not in good shape, and for me that meant that I was not going to be able to go on the family trip. My husband didn't want to go without me, but I convinced them to go and have fun.

They left for their trip on a Monday and headed into the mountains. They were fifteen minutes from the lodge, and that is when my world was turned upside down. It was snowing hard, and a huge truck crossed the yellow line and hit them head on. My entire family was killed on impact. The truck pushed my family over the rail and down the mountain. I received a phone call from a police officer, and after that everything was a blur. For the next year I was in a fog and never knew how to move forward. I tried to commit suicide five times. Three times I was rushed to the hospital. I actually died four times, and the last time I tried to kill myself, a nurse told me that I needed to stop, because God must have something for me to do (because I should have died).

I am not sure how this One Spark page got on my Facebook, but I am glad that it did. I read so many of the Sparks, and even went back years and read what I could read. I finally got the nerve to call One Spark and spoke to a woman for a while. Then she said, "Hold on a bit, our foundation's founder just walked in. I'm going to ask him to speak with you." Dave and I talked for over an hour. He told me that I needed to use my heartache from my family's death as a key instead of an anchor. I asked him what he was talking about, and that is when he explained it to me. Dave told me about his life filled with many heartaches and downright abuse. If you have not heard his story—wow—you need to hear it. After speaking with him, I knew that I had to move forward and leave the past in the past! He was very compassionate and loving, in a stern way. It was just what I needed.

I wanted to get my Spark on, and I knew just where to start. I decided to go through the rooms of my children and give away their belongings. I also did the same with my husband's things. You see, their rooms looked exactly the way they were the day they died. I made an effort to reach out to my children's friends first, and then I gave the items to the needy in my town. It was amazing how I felt as though there was a 10,000-pound weight lifted off my chest. The next thing I did was to start a support group for people who lost family. I never thought that I would ever have one person show up, and now we have fifteen people who are attending. I have used my pain to unlock their prison doors and help them move forward and start to live life again. I had so much guilt because I did not die with my family, and then I recalled what Dave said to me, "You need to realize that you did nothing wrong just because you lived." I now talk about this a lot to many people who have lost loved ones.

I want to thank every one of you for all the love you share on this page. Dave, thank you for all that you do and all that you did for me.

AIDS and Baby Jesus

"I have fought the good fight, I have finished the race, I have kept the faith." 2 Timothy 4:7 (NIV)

Hi. I want to tell you about a Spark I received from a stranger, and they told me all about One Spark while they were doing the Spark for me. I am a thirty-seven-year-old male who has been living with AIDS since I was twenty-five. I have been doing very well with the meds I have been on, and then one day they seemed to not be working, and I started to get sick. I needed help in my home with cleaning, laundry, and some cooking. When people came to my home, I felt that I needed to be up front with them. Well, as you can imagine, once they found out my condition, they were out of my home faster than the roadrunner could go. I had over twenty people come and talk about the job, and everything was okay until I told them I had AIDS.

I had all but given up on getting help, and then Rosa came to meet with me, and we had a great meeting. I was dreading telling her that I had AIDS, but I did and she said, "Okay, is that it?" I said, "Yes." Rosa replied, "Mr. Tim, I do not plan on trying to get you to switch teams, so I think we have nothing to worry about." She went on to tell me that she could see in my eyes that I found her 275 pounds of love attractive, but it would never be because she said she had been married for fifteen years. I started to laugh and then cry. She gave me a big hug and told me it would be okay. She asked about the pay and whether I was going to be able to pay her every week. I smiled and told her that I just sold a business that I had started and I did okay.

Rosa has been working for me for six months, and I would like to say that I have gotten better, but I have not. Rosa told me every day about the Spark club, as she called it. I asked her what it was, and that is when she showed me. Rosa asked me every day if I had my house in order, and I thought she meant where my money would go, until she asked me if I knew the baby Jesus. I said, "Not well," and she asked me if I wanted to meet him. I said, "Sure." Well, every single day Rosa talked about Jesus. And afterwards, (again every day) she would ask, "Now, do you have your house in order?" I thought she was crazy, but one day I knew what she was talking about, and so I did get my house in order.

My health is failing, and soon I will be with Jesus, and I am so happy. I have never been happier or more ready to meet Jesus. I have no family to speak of, because I was an only child and my dad died of cancer when I was only ten. Then I lost my mother when I turned thirty. I did not know what to do with my stuff, until one day I realized that Rosa and her family *were* my family. I made a will and have put Rosa's name on the deeds to my property, bank accounts, and titles to my autos.

The last thing we did was to get my funeral arrangements done, so she would not have to do it alone. I did all these things with Rosa to get my affairs ready and to make it easy for her when I died. She asked me, "Why do you do so many nice things for me?" I told her, "Because you are such a wonderful Spark in my life, Rosa." I told her that my biggest fear was to die alone—but that is no longer a fear of mine. I am so thankful that God brought her and her family into my life. I would have never gotten my house in order before I died, if it were not for her. Thank you, Rosa, for the wonderful, life-changing Spark you gave me.

Blind Man Anchor to Key (Lawyer)

"The blind see, the lame walk, the lepers are cured, the deaf hear, the dead are raised to life, and the Good News is being preached to the poor." Matthew 11:5 (NLT)

I have been blessed to meet you, my friend, and you are the one who has placed a Spark in my life. All that I am and all that One

Spark accomplishes in this world is because of God, and not me. Love, David A2J.

Being blind has made me work harder to fit in and to be able to be a productive person in the world. My parents never treated me any differently than my other brothers or sisters. They told me that if I want to succeed in life, I would have to work a little harder than the other person, because I was blind. That used to make me mad, until one day I realized that it was true. Then I knew what I had to do to become successful. I am a lawyer and think I am a very good one. I came to the realization years ago that if I wanted to be the best, I would have to work twice as hard as the next person. When I was employed at my first law firm, I quickly gained a reputation as one of the best lawyers there. I was not satisfied with just being the best lawyer; I wanted to be the best human being.

My wife found this One Spark page, and every night I listen to her as she reads the Sparks to me. I found it apparent to me that I have used what I thought was a curse as an anchor, instead of a key. Dave, this was not until my wife read me something you wrote about your life and how you chose to use what seemed as bad as a key to bless others. I told my wife that I would no longer use my disability as an anchor; I would use it as a key instead to give others the ability to move forward in their lives. I began to speak at churches and schools. I also contacted Dave to see if I could speak with him. We have spoken at a few schools and have many more scheduled for 2016. I am not writing about the Spark I did, but about the Spark that I was given through One Spark, to see my life as a key.

Sex Slave to Help Others

"However, he would not listen to her; since he was stronger than she, he violated her and lay with her." 2 Samuel 13:14 (NASB)

I wanted to thank you for helping me get out of the despair I was in. I am now seventeen and was taken when I was only thirteen. I cannot describe the misery I went through every day. I had to sleep with ten people a day, and now at the age of seventeen I will never have any chance of having a baby because my woman parts had to be removed. I wanted to die when I got out of there and now I want to live to help other girls who have gone through what I went through. You need to look up the facts on sex trafficking, post them on your Facebook, and make your children aware! We have to first educate people on what is going on and then we all need to agree that we will do our part. Then we need to join hands and bring these scumbags down.

NEW MOTHER HUSBAND DEPLOYED – CRYING BABY

"Love is patient, love is kind…" 1 Corinthians 13:4 (NIV)
I am a new mother, and when I say new, I mean twenty-two days new. I found out very quickly that being a mother is a hard job and there is no manual that comes with a new baby, like a new car. My husband was not there for the birth of our daughter because he has been deployed. I live over a 1,000 miles away from my parents and that has not been easy. My mother called and told me to bring her first grandbaby home. My parents purchased an airline ticket for Stacy and me. I was nervous about traveling with her for many reasons, but the biggest one was that I did not know how she would act on the flight. We were no sooner in our seats when Stacy started to cry, and I do mean cry. I tried everything I could think of, and still no luck. There was an older lady sitting next to me, and I thought she was upset because Stacy was crying, but she was not mad at all. She told me her name was Mildred and asked if she could try to calm Stacy. I said, "Yes, please!" It seemed that no sooner than Stacy was in her lap, she stopped crying. Mildred said, "Just relax now and rest—I have you covered."

I fought the sleep monster for what seemed like forever, but before I knew it, I was asleep. I slept the entire two-and-a-half-hour flight. I had not had a good rest since Stacy was born. I felt a light tug on my shirt, and when I woke up, Stacy was staring at me. Mildred handed Stacy to me and then asked where I lived. I told her, and the funny thing was that she lived less than a mile from me. We exchanged phone numbers and told each other we would talk soon.

When I returned home from visiting my parents, I called Mildred. She came over and we chatted like we had been friends forever. Mildred has become part of my family, and we have become part of hers. I have been on this One Spark page for several years and have always wished someone would Spark me. When they did, I did not think much about it, until one day I really started to think about what a Spark was. At that time, I realized that I had been given a huge Spark from Mildred.

Thank you, Mildred's friend.

Town's Favorite Son Marries Gay Girl: He Removed Her Anchor with Love

"Train up a child in the way he should go: and when he is old, he will not depart from it." Proverbs 22:6 (ESV)

I am a sixteen-year-old girl who is gay. I have struggled and actually tried to commit suicide three times because my peers were so mean to me. I had no friends at all. I live in a very small Christian town that loves the baby Jesus. I found that once I came out, all my friends came and went. The Assembly of God church pastor's son was our town's quarterback. He was a senior, already signed to play at the next level. He was our town's favorite son and a really nice guy. I had just been discharged from the hospital due to an attempted suicide, and he came to my house to talk to me. I thought he would be the last person who would want to be seen talking to me, because of being a Christian—I was wrong. He came in and we talked for a while. He asked me if I would go to the homecoming dance with him.

I sat there for a moment and then asked him, "Why would you want to take me?" He looked me in the eyes and said, "Because you are a beautiful young lady and I think you need a break." I said, "Yes, I'll go to the dance with you."

My mother and I travelled outside of town to look for a dress. We found the perfect one, and my mother told me that I looked beautiful in it. The night of our homecoming dance finally came, and my date arrived in a limo to pick me up. He came to the door and had a flower for me. He thanked my parents for allowing me to go with him and then asked what time I needed to be home. They told us and off we went to the prom. When we pulled up and he opened my door and I got out of the car, everyone was staring at us. He grabbed me, pulled me in close, and in we went. Many people approached him with varying requests, and even a few girls asked him to dance. He politely declined each time. For the first time in my life, I felt good about myself. We were at the dance for about an hour and he asked me if I wanted to get out of there to go have a soda. I said yes and off we went. We sat and talked for over three hours. I told him something that I had never told anyone—I was molested at the age of twelve by a neighbor boy. The boy's dad was my father's boss and the boy said that if I told anyone, he would have his dad fire my dad. I decided to keep it to myself. I grew to really hate boys. This kid, who was a year older than me lived next door, and so I had to see him every day of my life. As I looked up, I saw that my date had tears in his eyes. I asked him why and he said that he could feel my pain. He took me home that night, gave me a hug, and said to me, "That was the best date I've ever had in my life."

The following week when I saw him at school, he hugged me tight and said, "Thank you again for the date. Can we get together and hang out after school?" I said, "Yes." We met at his house where he introduced me to his parents, who were very nice. They thanked me for going to the dance with their son, and I thought, *It is me that should be thanking you!* We became the best of friends and spent all of our free time together. He went off to college, and we talked on the phone all the time.

His mother called me one day and said he had been in an accident on his way home to surprise me for my birthday. He fell asleep at the wheel. He was in the ICU, and when I got there, he looked terrible. I felt so bad that he was hurt because he wanted to surprise me on my birthday. I spent every day at the hospital. He had broken his leg very badly and was told he would not play football again. It broke my heart that the game he loved was taken from him because of me. After he told me to "Stop it with all that talk," he said, "When I get out of this hospital, you will have to drive me everywhere, because of my leg." He went on to tell me that he wanted to become a pastor like his father, because he loved the Lord and wanted to share his love with people. I said, "That's a wonderful idea; you'd be great at it!" About a month after he left the hospital, he asked me to drive him to our town's water falls. He said he needed to ask me something. I said okay, and off we went. As I said before, we are the best of friends. When we got there, he was acting funny, and I asked him what was wrong. He said, "Nothing." Then I really got scared that he was going to have another surgery to fix his leg. After a few minutes of small talk, I asked, "What is it that you want to ask me?" He yelled, at the top of his lungs, "Will you marry me?" He scared me so badly with his shouting, I just sat there. He looked so sad. I smiled and said, "Yes!" We both were incredibly happy.

That was eight years ago and we still are the best of friends. And, yes, he is a pastor. One thing I never knew was that One Spark had spoken at his college about the power of love and kindness and about what your legacy will be when you are through on this earth. He knew what he wanted to do, and he knew he wanted to do it with me. Dave and my husband talked for several hours about his life and how he handled all of his heartaches by turning them into keys. He went on to explain what that meant. I know now why he did not care about football. It was because he was going to use his heartache as a key to unlock someone's prison door. Trust me—my husband has used it with many people, and so have I. I have also used my story as a key to unlock many prison doors. You see, love is the key. We are not the moral judges of anyone, and that means we were put here to love one another—no matter what our differences may be. Love has the power to heal and to give hope. Dave, you have always said to us, "Whatever you do to change one life is worth it." I know many people do not see the work One Spark does and how it impacts so many lives, but we did and still do. We love you and One Spark. Never give up hope and never listen to people who say you are wasting your talent.

SEX TRAFFICKED – USES HER EXPERIENCE TO SAVE

"It would be better for them to be thrown into the sea with a millstone tied around their neck than to cause one of these little ones to stumble."
Luke 17:2 (NIV)

I was a victim of sex trafficking over eleven years ago. I was addicted to drugs, and one thing led to another. Before I knew it, I was working in spas and then got deeper into the web. I escorted, was pimped out, and walked the streets. I was lost for so long in the darkness, and I just gave up and gave into the pain. I was rescued by prayers of loved ones and by crying out to God on the floor of a crack house—He met me there!

The years that followed were so hard because I was always afraid and I did not dare trust men—any men! If I was in a group of people for too long and it was quiet, I had a panic attack and needed to make a quick exit. Before, when I was in the darkness, people intentionally got me high and did terrible things to me. I remember being so out of it and just lying there while these things happened to me; I pretended to be passed out because I didn't have the strength to fight.

I basically had to learn to think for myself again. I didn't realize how long it had been since anyone had asked me what I wanted instead of someone else deciding for me—years and years. There were a few times I returned to the clubs, partying, and sex because that was all I knew for so long! I am finally able to be independent with my thoughts and actions and don't have to keep asking people, "Is that okay?" before doing something. I finally know that I have more to offer this world than my body, and I can be around men and not think that's all they want. I still live in the same town where all the destruction and being trapped liked a prisoner took place. I drive along the streets I prostituted on every day.

All I can say is that the grace of God is more powerful than anything the enemy can ever do to us! I am so grateful that I was finally at a place in my life a few years ago where I could truly receive God's love—because to me, love was sex and I could not tell the difference. But one day He broke through and I felt love! I have never even sensed love from a man, so I am not sure if this is what it feels like, but I know it made me feel powerful—like I could do anything and still be comforted like a child, all at same time. The road to redemption and freedom, after you have been a prisoner in the drug and sex trade world, is a long and painful one. However, once you get past all the hurt and wounds you received and you're able to look in the mirror and not cry, you'll come to know freedom and the love of God in the purest sense!

Sex trafficking is a real, detrimental, horrific prison of torture that takes the victim and strips them of any kind of dignity, self-esteem, self-worth, and identity. Anything and everything that makes us human is taken away, and the victim is imprisoned and tortured repeatedly. We have to do more—so much more—than we are doing to help stop these animals that are in control of trafficking innocent, precious lives! It takes one flicker of hope to start a blaze of freedom through prayer and raising your voice!

STAR FOOTBALL PLAYER STANDS UP

"Speak up for those who cannot speak for themselves; ensure justice for those being crushed." Proverbs 31:8 (NLT)

I am fourteen years old and have a great home and lots of stuff. I am six feet two and I weigh 193 pounds. I am a starter on our football team, and kids at my school like me because I play sports. I love playing video games a lot; my mom and dad have good jobs and they get me the new games and boxes. There is a boy in my school who was getting picked on a lot because he was small and did not have good clothes. One day during class, a couple of boys were bugging a boy called James. I went over and told them to stop picking on him. They did stop and James and I became good friends. He helps me with my studies, and I teach him how to play video games. I make sure people know that he is my friend.

His mom got very sick and my parents helped care for her and James. They moved them into our home and I loved it. My parents did not want us to tell anyone because they did not want James to feel uncomfortable. James stayed in my room and we became like brothers. James would help me with the playbook and we loved each other.

When his mother got better, my parents suggested that she and James continue to stay with us. She told them she wanted to get back to her home. We are always with each other. I gave James my two game boxes and told him I would come to his home and play. James has not missed a game, and now he is the equipment manager on the team. I love him like my brother and he loves me the same. I hope the older people learn a lesson from our love—that is, you don't have to be the same, because we all have the same blood and come from the same God. I hope you like my Spark because James and I love yours.

In and Out of Jail – Twenty-Five Years of Prison

"Religion that God our Father accepts as pure and faultless is this: to look after orphans and widows in their distress and keep oneself from being polluted by the world." James 1:27 (NIV)

I have been in trouble since I was twelve years old. I have been in and out of jail. I am not yet thirty-five years old and I have three felonies. I felt as if I was never going to get my life straight. I have been told I am a good looking guy, with a great personality, but after a few minutes with me you knew you wanted nothing to do with me. That was until I met a man who told me that I needed to grow up and stop all my nonsense. I told him my story and that is when he stated that he had spent twenty-five years of his life in prison. He said he got caught up with the wrong crowd and was doing the wrong stuff. I said, "You got taken advantage of, bro." That is when he looked me in the eyes and said, "With all the stuff I've done over my life, I should've gotten life in prison."

He asked me if I needed a job, and I told him yes. He told me to meet him at 7 AM and be ready to work. We started our day by fixing a fence. While we were on the job, a lady asked him if he could look at her gate. He went over and put a few screws in it and tightened the bolts. She asked him how much money she owed, and he handed her a card. I thought, *What kind of scam is he running?* He was not running a scam at all; he handed her a One Spark card. I asked him what that was all about and he told me that it was about love. I knew it—this guy was a flower child or in some kind of cult.

It was mid-day and we went to pick up lunch—five of them! I said, "Bro, there are only two of us; who you giving the other three to?" He said, "You'll see." We made the first stop to a homeless lady. He gave her the food and one of those cards, and she gave him a big hug. We went to see two more homeless people and he did the same thing. I asked him, "Who pays you to do this?" He answered, "No one, and you need to learn how giving can change your life."

We got back to his work and he handed me a tablet. He then told me to read both the beginning story of One Spark and also all that was posted on their page. I laughed and said, "Sure." That is when he said to me, "You are a man of your word, right?" I said that I was. I got back to the house I was staying in, grabbed the tablet, and went directly to the One Spark page. I read the beginning story, and I have to say that it moved me. I then started to read about all the great things you people were doing. I found myself crying and I did not know why. I read stories until midnight. I could not wait to go to work the next day to ask my work buddy more questions.

I arrived at work and he asked me if I read what he asked me to read, and then he asked me what I had learned. I said, "There is big power in love and kindness." He said, "You are absolutely right." Then he told me that we had a few things to do before we got started working. We went to an older woman's house and changed some light bulbs. He didn't ask her to pay; he gave her a card instead. We went to a single mom's house and fixed her sink. And again he took no pay, but gave a One Spark card.

I could go on and on about my friend teaching me how to love and to be kind, but I need to bring this to a close. I have been working with my friend and mentor for four years now, and I love every minute of it. I met a lady who I fell in love with, and we are now married and expecting our first child. You see, what I learned is that when you love enough people, you will find someone who will love you.

NEGATIVE MOM – DAUGHTER UNCHAINED HER ANCHOR

"Her children rise up and bless her; her husband also, and he praises her, saying: 'Many daughters have done nobly, But you excel them all.' "
Proverbs 31:28–29 (NASB)

I have a fifteen-year-old daughter who loves to serve others. I am not sure where she got this from because my husband and I have never really been into serving others. She found your Facebook page about a year ago and has been in love with it ever since. She would come home after school and tell me that she was going to be working on some Sparks. I asked her what she meant and she told me all about the One Spark Foundation. I thought it was a good idea for her to get involved with this because it would make her a better person and teach her about giving.

She and her father are very close, and I have oftentimes been

129

jealous of the relationship they have because it was what I always wanted for myself when I was young. Her father would and will do anything with, or for her. They are the best of friends. Make no mistake about it, though, he is the one to discipline her. She came downstairs and told her dad what she was doing. Then she told him that she wanted him to go do Sparks with her. He asked her to explain what Sparks were. She did and he said, "I'm in!" I did not get invited because I am always negative—I call it being real. They went out and did ten Sparks. When they got home, they told me all about their experience. They both asked me to go with them the next time.

I became a very negative person after my oldest daughter died of cancer. It seemed as if my joy was stolen. I became very nasty and hard to get along with. I took my hurt out on my family, and they were the ones who loved me the most. The next day my daughter asked me to write kind notes to people we were going to give them to. I said, "I don't understand." She replied, "Tonight we are going to buy thirty roses, put them with the smiley face cards, and take them to people who have been there for us." She asked me to pour out my heart and allow the love of God to help me write the cards. You see, I turned my back on God when he did not heal my daughter. I had not been to church in five years.

I sat down at the table to start the project my daughter had entrusted to me. She said it was a job only I could do. She told me how much she and daddy loved me and that they could not wait to go Sparking with me that evening. I sat there for what seemed to be a year, and then I started to pour my heart out to the people who had been there for me through the loss of my daughter. I started with my mother-in-law and father-in-law. Next I moved on to my parents and then on to my many friends. When I was done, I had poured my heart out to thirty family members, friends, and other people who were there for me. I bought the roses and attached them to all of the cards my daughter gave me.

I married young and had always wanted several children, but

when my daughter died, that was it—I didn't want any more children. My husband begged me for another child, but I said no. The three of us delivered the Sparks, and many people cried when they read what I wrote to them. As they read the letters, I felt a burden lift off my heart, and there was a certain peace that came to me that I knew could only be from God. We have done many Sparks since that day, and our family is much stronger for it. I want to thank everyone who has sent in their Sparks, because they have changed me. With your words of love and encouragement my family has blessed many. One last thing—I am pregnant with twins. Thank you, Dave for all you do. I know it is hard at times, but please never get weary— because my family and the world need you.

Stuck in the Mud – Sparks are Keys

"Give to everyone who asks you, and whoever takes away what is yours, do not demand it back." Luke 6:30 (NIV)

I wanted to tell the people who stopped and helped get our car out of the mud, thank you. I am a mother of three little kids and my husband is deployed. I was taking my kids to lunch when I hit a puddle of water, and that made me go off the road into the ditch. The ditch had a lot of water in in, and my car sank deep into the mud. I got out and tried to flag several cars, but no one wanted to stop. I guess I looked a little crazy. After about an hour, a family pulled up in a big truck and asked me if they could help me. I said, "I hope so, because I am stuck in the mud." The dad and two boys immediately surveyed the situation, and then the dad got back in his truck and the boys took a rope down to my car. The boys hooked it to my car and then asked if I minded if they drove the car out of the ditch. I said, "Yes, that would be fine." In a flash, my car was out on the road again.

I got into my car and grabbed my wallet so I could pay them. They asked if my husband was a marine. I said, "Yes," and the father replied, "So is our son. He is overseas now, and we pray for his safety every day. We don't want your money, but we'd like to give you something instead." He handed me a One Spark card and then told me that they would be praying for my husband. I gave them all hugs and we left. I had such a warm feeling in my heart from the kindness that this family gave my family. I do not have a lot, but I promise that I will be a Spark person for life.

Love, In the mud no more.

SPARKED AT GARAGE – SPARK IS THE KEY

"He who gives to the poor will never want, but he who shuts his eyes will have many curses." Proverbs 28:27 (ESV)

I am a single mother of four. Times have been tough, but we seem to make it every day. I focus on having an attitude of gratitude rather than one of 'poor me.' I had to take my car to the mechanic to get it worked on because it was not running right. They told me that I needed a timing belt, brakes, spark plugs, and several other things. I walked in to the office to go over the estimate, and when the owner told me how much it was going to be, I started to cry. The bill was going to be almost one thousand dollars. I said, "I do not have that kind of money, so I will not be able to have you fix it." He asked me if I could continue to use the car I was currently driving, and I said yes. I was borrowing it from my mother, and she had another car to drive in the meantime.

Several days had gone by, and I had not heard from anyone at the garage about my car, so I gave them a call. The owner told me that my car would be done in the morning. The next day my mother drove me to the shop. I went in to speak with the owner to find out what I was going to have to do. He said to me, "A man happened to overhear our earlier conversation about you not being able to afford to repair your vehicle, and he told me to fix everything that was wrong with it." I could not believe what he was telling me! He then took me out to see my car. It had new tires and brakes, an oil change, new plugs, a transmission flush, a coolant flush, timing belt change, shocks, and much more. I just stood there and began to cry; the owner gave me a hug. I asked, "Why me?" He answered, "Why *not* you?" To this day I do not know who my car angel was, but I want them to know that I will never forget what they did and that I have passed on the Spark they gave to me and my family many times. I went straight home to look up what One Spark was, and I fell in love with the concept immediately. I will continue to Spark until the day I die.

Love, Driving safe.

Trafficked at Only Twelve

"He heals the brokenhearted and bandages their wounds." Psalm 147:3 (NLT)

Sex trafficking is a form of modern-day slavery in which individuals perform commercial sex through the use of force, fraud, or coercion. Minors under the age of eighteen engaging in commercial sex are considered to be a part of human trafficking, regardless of the use of force, fraud, or coercion. Sex traffickers frequently target victims and then use violence, threats, lies, false promises, debt bondage, or other forms of control and manipulation to keep victims involved in the sex industry for their own profit. Sex trafficking exists within diverse and unique sets of venues and businesses including: fake massage parlors, escort services, residential brothels, public city streets, truck stops, strip clubs, hostess clubs, hotels and motels, and elsewhere.

Hi, my name is Holly, and no, Holly is not my real name. I want to tell you about my nightmare called sex trafficking. I was a normal twelve-year-old who loved to be outside with my friends. I loved to play and just have fun. I have blonde hair and blue eyes. That made me a perfect target to be taken. I remember being outside, walking

133

to my friend's house, when a van pulled up. In a split second, I was gone—no, not on vacation, but to what I later would call a nightmare on earth. In twenty-four hours I was over 1,000 miles away from home. I was scared and did not know what to do. They told me that if I did not do exactly what they said, they would kill my entire family.

The second day I had my first encounter with a man in his fifties. He was mean, and there was absolutely nothing off limits. I was in so much pain, and I wanted to die. That's when they gave me meth for the first time. It numbed me and let me get through each day without the pain. At the age of only twelve, I was required to sleep with as many as ten men a day. I was taken to many major events where the men would flock in, wanting to hit the twelve-year-old. Every one of them knew my age, and I always thought, *Would you like this to happen to your daughter?* I knew not to say anything to anyone, because every day some girl was either getting beaten, having her fingers broken, or starved—to the point of almost dying.

One day, a group of men kicked in our door and took seventeen of us girls to safety. I remember holding on to one of the men so tightly and not wanting to let him go. We jumped into a van and headed off to safety, only to have the van break down. I was crying so hard and praying that we would not be found. The van started moving again, and they got us to safety. I am now eighteen years old. I've had a full hysterectomy. I also have a colostomy bag that will be with me for the rest of my life.

You see, I was from a small town where things like this are not supposed to happen—but they did. I write this letter to warn you to be on the lookout for girls out at night, girls being transported together, and boys calling on your daughter, or any other thing that just does not seem right. You need to be on your children's Facebook, Twitter, or any other social media. It does not matter if they like it or not; it is for their own protection. There are thousands of children who are sold into slavery each year. What can you do? Post this, repost it, and continue to post information about sex trafficking in the United States. It is over a thirty billion dollar industry, right here in our country. It is not the horrible things bad people do that is ruining our country, it is the good people who see bad things but do nothing.

To the ordinary men who risked their lives to free us, I want to say thank you. I will never know your names, but I know your hearts. To the people who believe in prayer, hit your knees and pray for the safety of every person who is a slave to be rescued and healed. I am often asked if I will be all right, and my answer is, "Through the grace of God and the love of my family, I will be." But, it's not enough to simply ask, "Will you be okay?" The real question is, "How many more children will be taken in order to get your attention?"

I hope that you will not be like my parents and not care until it happens to you or someone you know. This, again, is a thirty-plus billion dollar industry in the United States and over a one hundred billion dollar industry worldwide. I wish I could play for you the video that repeats in my mind—of what happened to me—because I promise you, it would make you sick. I was only a child. There are over 100,000 new people trafficked a year. How many people will it take for you to get involved???

LOST SON AND HUSBAND – HELPS WITH GRIEVING PROGRAM

"Blessed are those who mourn, for they will be comforted." Matthew 5:4 (NIV)

The last year was a blur to me because I lost my son in an automobile accident and then my husband to a heart attack. They were my life. My husband wanted many children, but that was not in the cards for me. I had Bo, and then could not have any more children. The three of us did everything together. My son had just graduated from high school and was excited about going to college. My husband and I would always wait up for Bo to get home from work, and then we would talk about what had happened that day. I think the best time of our day was when we were able to hear about

Bo's day. Bo could have gone out with friends or go to his room after his work day. But he didn't because he knew how much we loved to sit and talk with him. If he was going to do something or go somewhere, he would tell us.

He was an hour late coming home one evening, and my husband and I were getting very worried. My husband called his phone, and there was no answer. Just as my husband and I were heading out to look for him, there was a knock on the door. It was a friend of ours, the sheriff of our small town. He looked terrible and was having a hard time speaking. That is when my husband asked him if something had happened to Bo. He said, "I am sorry, but Bo was killed in an auto accident. He was on the way home and hit a deer, and then his truck overturned. When I arrived a little bit after the accident, Bo was still alive. We did everything we could to save him. I held his hand and he told me to tell you that he loved you and would see you in heaven. My husband collapsed and had to be rushed to the hospital. He had a mild heart attack and was told to take it easy. The loss of our son was more than he could bear and three weeks later he had a massive heart attack and died.

Here is my Spark. We donated all the organs from my son and husband, and there are eleven people who are in a better place because of the donation. I met the young man who received Bo's heart, and he is a nice boy. He is seventeen, and if he would not have received a new heart, he would have died. You see, I would have never given up the organs if my son had not told my husband and me that he wanted to be an organ donor in the event of his death. I help out with a grieving program, and I believe that my story has helped so many people move on to use their loss as an opportunity to be a blessing rather than a curse.

Thank you very much for this One Spark page. Dave, once you asked if One Spark really matters—Honey, without this page I would have committed suicide for sure. So please never doubt what you have created with the guidance of God. There may be people who doubt it, mock you, and say your life is a waste, but I am proof that what you and God have created does matter and is making a big difference.

WAS GIVEN TIRES AND THEN GAVE TIRES

"And God is able to bless you abundantly, so that in all things at all times, having all that you need, you will abound in every good work." 2 *Corinthians 9:8 (NIV)*

I don't know if you remember me or not, because I know you help many people. I am the woman who you bought tires for and ice cream for my children. I have not written to say thank you because I was waiting to get on my feet to pass on a Spark. I have now graduated from nursing school and have a great job at a local hospital.

One night I had to work late and was leaving to go home, when I walked out of the hospital and saw a woman whose car had a flat tire. She told me that she did not have any money to repair it. I sat there for a moment and then told her that she would not be able to get the tire fixed tonight, but she could in the morning. I looked at the tire and knew it could not be repaired because the cords were showing. She started to cry and then said, "I do not know what I am going to do." I told her I had a friend who could pick up the car, find a used tire for her, and not charge her. She said, "Really?" I smiled and said, "Yes."

The next morning I called a local tire store and told them what was going on. I said, "I would like to buy four new tires for her." The man on the other end of the phone asked if it was a joke, and I told him no. The man asked for the tire size so he could at least bring a tire to put on in order to drive the car to the shop. I went up to her husband's hospital room and told her that my friend needed her keys. I added that I would make sure the car got back to her ASAP. I handed the keys to the owner of the car shop, and he told me what a great person I was. I relayed to him my story regarding One Spark buying tires for my own car. He told me that was great, and then took off with the car.

About three hours later he called me to let me know he was finished with the car. I went to pick it up and he said, "Her car has new brakes and I changed the oil for free." I replied, "I'll pay for it now." He then said, "Oh, no, I want IN on this Sparking." I took the car back to the woman and told her the tire was fixed. She thanked me profusely. She did not check the car out then because her husband had just come out of surgery. I did not have a work shift that particular day, so I did not see her later on. The next morning when I came in, she was waiting at the front door of the hospital. She began to cry and said, "Thank you so very much!" I told her that the mechanic changed her brakes and gave her an oil change for free.

David and One Spark, you have started a fire in my heart that will never go out. I will be a Spark Giver until the day I die.

HUMBLED BY HANDICAPPED VETERAN

"Blessed are those who hunger and thirst for righteousness, for they will be filled." Matthew 5:6 (NIV)

I walked out of Walmart today and got in my car. As I began to pull out, I had to wait for a man in a wheelchair to pass by. As I watched him, I noticed that he was missing his right leg from the knee down and was wearing what appeared to be old, government issued combat boots. He was (from my guess) in his late sixties/early seventies and seemed to be stopping to take a break. He had not realized that I had started my car and was attempting to pull out, so when he saw me, he waved in an apologetic manner and rolled forward three more times in his wheelchair and then took another break. I backed my car up the inches I had previously pulled forward, put it in park, turned off the engine, and got out. I walked up to him and introduced myself. I asked him if I could assist him with his shopping and he, quite grumpily, said that he was doing just fine and was not getting much anyway.

I (being my usual stubborn self) insisted and proceeded to push him and tell him a little about myself. He interrupted me and said that he only needed help to the door, to which I picked up where I had left off before he interrupted me. I told him about Fayetteville, my horses, and my nephews (I had parked a good ways away from the front doors). And when I reached the entrance, I continued to push him and talk. We reached the produce area and I asked him to tell me about himself. He reluctantly looked at me and began telling me that he lived in Sod-Lincoln County and that he recently lost his wife. I asked him if he was a veteran, to which he replied that he was, but with pain on his face, so I changed the subject and asked if he had made a shopping list. He handed me a list with only four items on it: peanut butter, soup, bread, and bananas. So we began shopping and I continued to talk—hard to believe—I know.

Once we had chosen the items on his list, I asked if he needed any essentials, such as milk, eggs, and butter. He said, "I might not make it home before those go bad." "How did you get here, to the store?" I asked. He told me that he did what he was doing in the parking lot until he got to Route 119 and then hitchhiked with a trucker to the parking lot. So I called a taxi for him and grabbed the essentials (plus a few other things) and put them in the cart. After placing a gallon of milk in his basket as well, I noticed he was crying. People were passing by us, looking sideways at him. I knelt down and asked him what was wrong and he replied, "You are doing far too much for an old man you barely know." I said, "Well, where I am from, and from the family I was raised in, we help one another, no matter the task. I have never met a stranger. You deserve everything I am doing for you because you fought for my freedom and sacrificed so much."

We made it to the checkout line and I paid for his groceries, against his protests. When we got outside, we waited for the taxi together. He thanked me over and over again and appeared (to me) to have been in a much better mood than when I found him. When the taxi arrived, I helped him load his groceries and wheelchair into the vehicle and asked the driver to take him home and help him into his house with his bags. I gave him the only cash I had on me—forty-four dollars—also against his will. I said, "Thank you for your service," before closing the car door. Once again tears formed in his eyes. He thanked me one last time and said, "God bless you." I returned to my car and could not help but cry.

This is the world we live in today. How many people passed by him and would have continued to ignore him while he struggled? How many people are willing to give their money to Vanity Fair to read all about Bruce Jenner but not help a veteran pay for his groceries? Today was a truly humbling experience for me, and I consider myself extremely blessed to have the capability of understanding what is truly important in this world. THAT man was a HERO, and far too many may say otherwise. I am sorry that this post was so long, and if you have read it to this point, I hope you are as humbled as I was. God bless the men and women who have fought for our right to view the wrong people as heroes, and thank God for the people who know better.

FENCES DON'T MAKE GOOD NEIGHBORS

"The second is this: 'Love your neighbor as yourself.' There is no commandment greater than these." Mark 12:31 (NIV)

We recently acquired a Rottweiler puppy, and we were informed that we would have to raise our fence on one side of our backyard to prevent the dog from jumping over it. At the time, it was a chain link fence, making it easy for our neighbor to visit with our dogs she enjoyed so much. She also loved conversing with our toddler and watching him on his trampoline. And, of course, it made it easier for the two of us to chat. She's an older woman who lives alone—so kind and thoughtful—making for a great neighbor.

I wasn't too excited about having a fence built, to say the least. When I went out to the yard to check the building progress, I was not happy. With a lump in my throat and a tear in my eye, I told my husband that I did not like it! I didn't relish the idea of our neighbor coming out of her home, having only a fence to stare at, and feeling separated from us. It broke my heart. Well, the guys were almost down to the last foot of fence being put up. They had been there for two days.

I figured my husband would just roll his eyes and let it be. Instead, he informed the workers of my concern. After discussing it a bit, one of the workers noticed our neighbor in her yard and relayed my feelings. We all met at the middle of the fence and they started taking down the planks. There stood my neighbor, all choked up, wiping tears from her eyes. The workers cut about five feet of fence down to a waist-high level. She said, "I can't believe you are doing this for me!" We did it for all of us. I may have suggested the Spark, but my husband put it into action—and those great workers made it happen. Who says high fences make good neighbors?

Teenager Sparked a Mother – Sparks Aren't Forgotten

"Do nothing out of selfish ambition or vain conceit. Rather, in humility value others above yourselves." Philippians 2:3 (NIV)

There was a woman in Walmart who was buying groceries. When the cashier told her that she owed fifty-seven dollars, the woman replied that she only had about twenty-four dollars. She told the cashier to just go ahead and start removing some food items until she would have enough money to pay for everything. Behind the woman was a sixteen-year-old girl who had just worked for her dad landscaping the day before, and she said to the cashier, "No, wait a minute… how much more does she need?" The cashier answered, "Thirty-three dollars." The sixteen-year-old handed the cashier forty dollars and said that she would pay for the rest of the woman's groceries. The teenager then asked the cashier not to put the items back. The lady, attempting to buy the groceries, said, "It's okay; I don't want you to do that." However, the teenager insisted, and the woman thanked her before she left the store.

The person who posted this was talking about her niece and how much it touched her heart to see her give the money—she worked so hard for—to a stranger in need. She went on to tell how the teenager bought two things for herself with the money she had left: cookies and deodorant (lol). It touched my heart to read of a youngster being so thoughtful and giving to a perfect stranger, but it made my heart smile even more knowing that teenager was my daughter! P.S. She had made fifty dollars from working for her dad the day before.

Eleven-Year-Old with Asperger's Cut Hair For Kids with Cancer

"Peace I leave you; my peace I give you. I do not give to as the world gives. Do not let your heart be troubled and do not be afraid." John 14:27 (NIV)

My eleven-year-old daughter (who has Asperger's) has never had a haircut—well, nothing more than a trim done at home. She had extreme anxiety about people touching her hair. A few months ago, she learned of children needing wigs, due to the effects of cancer treatments. She then decided to donate her hair. I told her to think about it for a while, and after two months she decided she definitely wanted to do it.

After much anxiety, she finally made it to the salon. The stylists were very busy and we had to wait. This only heightened her anxiety, but she was adamant. Finally, it was her turn. The woman who had just finished having her hair done looked at my girls and asked which of them was donating her hair, as my daughter was the buzz of the salon. She approached my daughter and said, "This is a truly kind and brave thing you're doing. Since you are making such a selfless donation, I would like to make one too." The woman then pulled a twenty-dollar bill out of her purse and handed it to my daughter. My daughter, of course, refused to take it, and looked to me for guidance. The woman then got down low, to my daughter's eye level, and explained to her that her nine-year-old niece had cancer, and because of donations was able to receive a wig and feel like a normal little girl again. She took my daughter's hand and placed the money in it, saying that she was simply paying for the wig of another child with cancer. We were all in tears by this point. We both hugged this kind woman and she left.

My daughter ended up donating eleven and a half inches of her beautiful hair. What came after was just as amazing. My daughter told me that she didn't want to keep the money. She wanted to pay it forward again. She decided to go to the pet store and purchase some food and toys and place them in the collections box to go to our local animal shelter. I have never been more proud of my child!

THE PRODIGAL SON

"For this son of mine was dead and is alive again; he was lost and is found. 'So they began to celebrate.' " Luke 15:24 (NIV)

I stopped at Kroger a little while ago to grab something to snack on. I left the store and there was this kid (I say kid because he was considerably younger than I) up against the building, all hunched up and cold. He asked me if I had a couple of dollars so he could go across the street to get some soup at the Chinese place. I could see he was most likely serious and really just wanted something to eat. He was soaking wet and shaking. I said, "Come with me." We got in my car and drove to the Chinese restaurant. I asked him what he wanted and he said, "Soup is more than enough." In addition to the soup, I bought him beef and broccoli with house fried rice. We asked for the food to go and walked down to the laundromat a few doors down, where I paid for him to throw his soaked clothes in the dryer (he had some sweatpants and a t-shirt in his bag to put on in the meantime).

This kid told me how he was about to give up hope of anyone actually helping him out. He said that he had gotten into a fight with his dad and left home, catching a ride to Bloomington with a couple of friends. "They left me here," he said. He continued with, "I've been sleeping under the bridge where the storm drain runs under the train tracks by BroMenn. I don't know anyone in Bloomington and I don't have any money. I don't think my dad wants me to come back home." After he finished his food, I asked for his father's phone number and then called him. A woman answered the phone, and I asked if she knew this boy (name withheld for privacy) and she started crying and yelling for her husband. When he got on the phone, I described our evening to him. I told him where we were, and his dad arrived about a half hour later. He never had a harsh or upsetting thing to say to his boy; he just hugged him very tightly and simply said, "Let's go home." The dad thanked me and offered to give me some money for helping his son, but I refused.

As they began to back the car out, the father put on the brakes, and his son got out. He came up to me and shook my hand. Then he said, "Last night, while I was sitting under the bridge, God told me that an honest man with a heart of gold would save me soon." With that, he thanked me and left with his father. I think it might be time to brush a little of the dust off that book I used to cherish so long ago.

Jammies In Memory

"And we know that in all things God works for the good of those who love him, who have been called according to his purpose." Romans 8:28 (NIV)

Six years ago, I lost two nephews within four days of each other. This came upon the heels of losing three other relatives in a fourteen-month period. These two boys were children. Ian died on February 19th at the age of seven. We lost him to brain cancer. Garrison died on February 23rd—taken by his mother's hand—at the age of seventeen months old. For a long time I dreaded February—hated it—and just wanted that month over.

I decided to do something constructive, in the names of the

boys, so I could heal. So I went out to lunch with a few girlfriends. Afterwards, we donated stuffed animals to the San Diego Children's Hospital and jammies for foster children. The first year we had six pairs of jammies and eight stuffed animals. The next year I proposed the idea to all my friends, and they overwhelmed me—sixty-five pairs of jammies to foster kids and sixty-five stuffed animals, half of which went to the Sherriff's department, to give to kids in accidents or being taken from an abusive situation, and half to San Diego Children's Hospital. This year we gathered 240 jammies and 216 animals, and a few more are still on the way. In their names, Ian Henderson and Garrison Burchett, we are doing well. I took pain and made it joy, and look what my friends and I have done!

Ran Away at Twelve

"Be sure of this: The wicked will not go unpunished, but those who are righteous will go free." Proverbs 11:21 (NIV)

Hi One Spark. I am twenty-five years old, and at the age of twelve I ran away from home because I was physically abused by my mother's boyfriend. I never thought that anything in the outside world could be worse than where I was living. By the third night on the streets, I was hungry and cold and had no one to turn to. A young, handsome guy walked up to me and told me that he was going to be my prince charming. He said he'd take care of me and love me forever. Right—he loved me as long as I was producing income for him. The first time I became a problem to him, I received a severe beating and wound up in the hospital. I was asked by the hospital workers what happened. I told them that I was in a gang and I got beaten for initiation. I was sold over ten times to ten different men to make income. I would have sex anywhere from fifteen to twenty-five times a night. I never thought it would be possible to get away from those hateful, disgusting people.

One night I met a woman who told me she could help me get away from those men. I was so scared, but I had nothing to lose because I was to the point where I just wanted to die. The lady told me her story of how she was bought and sold as a commodity item for over twelve years. We made arrangements for a point in time in which she would pick me up. I looked forward to leaving that disgusting world forever. She was right on time, but the only thing we did not anticipate was my pimp showing up. He grabbed me and started hitting me; the lady jumped out and tried to defend me. He punched her in the face. That is when an innocent bystander jumped in, pulled a gun on the guy, and told him to leave me alone. Little did we know that he was an off-duty police officer.

My pimp was arrested and spent nine days in jail. Then, of course, he was back on the streets doing what he had done before to so many innocent young girls, and even some young boys. I was in desperate need of medical attention, clothing, dental work, and many other things. My friend called the founder One Spark to ask if there was anything he could do to help provide the necessary assistance I needed. She came back and told me that One Spark was going to pay for everything I needed.

That is when I met Dave and—WOW—what an awesome guy. He told me that that he loved me and that everything would be all right. I said to him, "That is easy for you to say, because you have never been through what I have been through." That is when Dave told me that he had been molested and sold as a child. He said, "You need to use this situation as a key to unlock someone else's prison door." He spent the next four and a half hours speaking to me about what he had been through in his own life. I have to admit that I felt so much better about my own. I speak to Dave on a daily basis, and we have made a pledge together to stop the buying and selling of people in the world. I made a promise to be the voice for those who have none.

JAMIE

"As iron sharpens iron, so one person sharpens another." Proverbs 27:17 (NIV)

I met a little boy, named Jamie, several years ago who caused me to want to keep striving for the moon, instead of only hitting a fence post. One night I was working with an older gentleman named Fred on one of the rescue wagons. I've always said this man walks closer to God than anyone I have ever met. I was so tired that I began to pray that no one else would need our assistance. I asked Fred, "Would you please say a little prayer that no one else needs our help tonight?" He answered, "Nope, God has a plan for us."

We started down the road when it began to pour rain, and then I realized I did not have my rain gear. I looked up ahead and there was a broken-down car. I pulled in behind the car. Darn it! It was raining, and I was just getting over the crud. I did not want to help the people in that car. I said to Fred, "You take care of this one." He replied, "Nope, God wants you to handle it." I got out, walked over to the car, and asked if they needed assistance. A little boy piped up, "Well, we have a flat and I think we need help...just kidding!" I was so mad—I was wet, cold, feeling sorry for myself, and just wanted to go home.

I got the jack out and went to work on the tire. It seemed like it took forever; I finally finished changing the tire an hour later. I knocked on the driver's side window and then handed the boy's mother a One Spark card. Then this little boy said to me, "I want to have a meeting with you tomorrow—it's life or death." In my mind I thought, *I wish it were me who was going to die.* I started to walk back to my vehicle. The little boy got out of his car and yelled, "I want to meet with you!" I answered, "Okay."

The next morning at 8 AM he called the One Spark office to inquire about setting up a meeting with me; it was to be at 2 PM. I drove to his house, knocked on the front door, and found this little boy dressed in a suit. I was wearing shorts. As he showed me to his "office," he said, "Nice of you to take this meeting seriously." While

147

pulling back a sheet that hid the dining room, he told me to have a seat. Jamie said, "When I was little—" I interrupted him and asked, "How old are you?" "Almost seven," he answered. He continued with, "The reason I asked you here was to tell you that God said you were going to help pay off this house for my mom." I exclaimed, "WHAT!?" He said, "I don't want money from you, but you need to take me to five of your friends. One of them will pay it off." I was so mad that I shot back, "I am done here!" and got up to leave. Jamie said this one last thing to me, "Until you do this for me, you won't sleep very well." I retorted, "I don't anyway." I left that day so angry that a little boy could do that to me.

I believe there are three types of people in this world: the first person who listens to the soft voice of God; another who needs to be yelled at; and the third person who has to be hit over the head with a baseball bat in order to get their attention. That last one is me. Approximately three months later, I found myself hardly sleeping at all. And, when I finally did drift off to sleep, I heard Jamie saying to me, "Listen to God." I called him and said, "Okay, I'm ready to have you meet my contacts, but I want to let you know that three of the five are just people I do business with—I wouldn't say that we are friends." Jamie replied, "That's okay, because one of them will pay off my mom's house before I die."

I picked Jamie up in my black corvette that he said was the bat mobile. We were on a mission. We went into the first office, just long enough for me to make the introductions. Jamie said, "No, this person is not the right one." "Jamie, we have to sit and talk about this," I replied. He repeated his negative findings again at the second, third, and fourth stops. When we walked into the very last office, Jamie asked if he could sit down. The owner of the office (Mr. X) was very, very rich—and not very nice. Jamie jumped right into his story and then continued with, "You are going to pay off my mom's house because she has not been able to work because I have cancer. My dad left us because he could not handle me being sick." Mr. X asked, "How much?" Jamie replied, "One hundred forty-eight thousand, one hundred seventy-five dollars and eighty-seven cents." I could tell that this man (who I do a lot of business with) was very angry. Jamie said, "Thank you for your time. I need to tell you something. Until you pay off my mom's house, you won't sleep much and you will have bad dreams."

When Jamie walked out of the office, Mr. X laid into me and asked, "Why did you bring this kid to my office?" I told him that I had not been able to sleep. Mr. X proceeded to call me names I can't repeat and told me to get out. I complied, and Jamie and I headed for the car. Jamie said, "Do you want to bet ten dollars that he will pay off my mom's house?" I answered, "Yeah, but you are going to lose." He asked me if he could hold the ten spot because I looked a bit shady. I said, "Yes, you can."

Five months later, Jamie called and told me to get in my bat mobile and pick him up. He said, "Frogs are flying at 500 miles per hour and the devil called me and said his pit froze over." You see, I had told Jamie that the only way this house would be paid off by Mr. X was if those three things happened. We went to the office and after we were seated, I looked at Mr. X and asked him, "Are you okay?" He said, "No, because I can't sleep and I keep having these bad dreams." I started to give Mr. X a hard time about paying off the house because he could not sleep, and then I realized I better be quiet.

Jamie was now eight, and the cancer was getting the best of him. I went to the hospital every day and lay in bed with him. He would rub my head and then we both would fall asleep. Mr. X grew to love this little boy as much as I did. Jamie asked him if he would look after his mom when he passed away. Mr. X said, "You'll be here longer than me." Jamie's reply was, "No, Jesus needs me in heaven."

Jamie absolutely loved baseball. I was able to give Jamie a signed baseball from a guy I knew from our college team. Soon after, we received a phone call informing us that Jamie had taken a turn for the worse and we needed to get to the hospital. Mr. X and I went to see him. Jamie had asked to be taken off the pain meds so he could think. He showed us his baseball and what was written on it: LISTEN

TO DAVE, KEEP YOUR PANTS UP, AND WHEN YOU HIT THE HOME RUN TODAY, I WILL LINE UP THE ANGELS AND HAVE THEM CHEER. I stayed for about two hours and then left to allow his mom time to be with him.

Jamie had told me, "Jesus is coming to get me at noon, Dave, and he won't be late." I smiled and said, "I love you, Jamie; you have changed my life." I left with the ball in my hand and went to my office. Jamie's mother called me later and told me he had passed at 11:01 AM. He wanted me to know that he loved me and that Jesus was not late. He died at 11:01 AM! If I had not moved from thinking all about me to thinking only about him, I would have missed the best friend and gift I will ever have. I love you buddy. Hit a home run for me in heaven.

David L. Hill

SAVED HIS LIFE

"A person finds joy in giving an apt reply – and how good is a timely word!" Proverbs 15:23 (NIV)

Encouragement, a warm heart, and acts of kindness can be incredibly powerful. In fact, they might just save a life! This was sent to us from a One Spark friend.

My mother was given a note yesterday from a customer at her work. She said the customer had been having a rough time recently, and she had been encouraging him. He wrote this note on an old Christmas card turned inside out: YOU SAVED MY LIFE.

MARY, THE DOG IN GEORGIA

"For every beast of the forest is mine, the cattle on a thousand hills. I know the birds of the hills, and all that moves in the field is mine." Psalm 50:10-11 (NIV)

I feel like it's a Spark that will change this little girl's life. I'm a trucker by trade, but I also transport rescued shelter pets to their adopters across the country, at no charge. This one touched my heart and many others as well. This Spark is about Britt; she is fourteen years old and has autism. For a long time, Britt had her eye on a dog that was rescued from a puppy mill. Mary (the dog) went to a rescue shelter in Georgia. For months, Britt and her mom, Amy, couldn't find a way to get Mary to them in Illinois. That's where I came in. I read their plight and was contacted through a friend about Britt and Mary. I knew in my heart I couldn't let this girl down.

I planned my route so that I could pick up Mary in Georgia. I finally was able to get Mary, and off we rode. Because it was near a holiday, I had to hold onto Mary until I could plan a trip to Illinois. We didn't tell Britt that Mary was coming. We wanted it to be a surprise, and it was. I met Amy and Britt this past Sunday, and just seeing this young girl touched my heart. The joy on this girl's face is irreplaceable; it's a Spark for me that has shot me through the clouds. The happiest part is that Mary doesn't even know she will be assisting Britt in her everyday life. That's right—Mary will go for training to assist Britt every day, even in school. Gosh, this warms my heart every time I talk about it.

Dilemma

ELECTRIC BILL PAID

"so that your giving may be in secret. Then your Father, who sees what is done in secret, will reward you." Matthew 6:4 (NIV)

I just want to tell you how inspired I am, on a regular basis, by the things I read and see that you all do to help others on this One Spark site. I have been following you for a while, and I love to see the amazing ways God works through us in this world. I had a similar situation about three months ago at the electric company. I am thirty-seven years old and a mother of a five-year-old boy and two girls, ages two and four.

I have continually been employed since I was of age, but last summer I began to have problems, and eventually was no longer able to work. I have been diagnosed with a systemic disease that affects my autonomic nervous system, which in turn affects most of my body. It is destroying my bone mass and makes my heart race. Sometimes I come close to passing out, among many other things. I also have a rare tumor disorder. To say the least, it has been taxing.

My husband was arrested two years ago due to someone falsely accusing him of something terrible. Because of extenuating circumstances and a lack of information, he was blindsided and sentenced to eight years in prison. We are now trying to prove this case and reverse the horrible damage that has been done, but considering my situation, it is very difficult (financially). I have applied for disability, but I am still awaiting the decision. The last few months have been especially difficult, and I have struggled to pay my bills. (Even as I write this, I am online searching for a hidden resource I haven't used to pay my electric bill that is scheduled for disconnect tomorrow.)

I took my daughters, as well as all the cash I had, with me to the electric company. I spoke to the cashier and asked her if I could wait to pay the last sixty dollars of the bill for a few more days without loss of service (and a hefty eighty-dollar reconnect charge). She said, "That will be fine." There was a nice man in the lobby, awaiting his turn. He was talking to my girls, smiling and waving at them and being silly.

The next day, I went back to take them another twenty dollars and ask for more time for the rest, and they told me that I didn't owe anything else on that bill. I was very confused, and I asked her to check again. The last thing I wanted was to think it was okay and then—boom—be without electricity. While she was double checking for me, the cashier who had served me the day before came to the window, smiled, and said, "Ms. Martinez, an anonymous payer took care of the rest of your account, so you are good until next month." I was speechless, breathless, and started to cry. I had no other words besides, "Wow, thank you so much!" I know it must have been that nice man in the lobby. Who else could it have been? No one else knew my situation. I often wish I could hug his neck and tell him thank you so much. No one has EVER in my life done something like that for us.

Since that day, even if I'm struggling, I try to remember that God is an on-time God, and I try to have faith. I may be at the end of my rope—like I said, right now I am in dire straits—but I see the world around me and the good things that people are doing for others, and I am inspired. Thank you so much for providing this for people. Thank you for reminding the world that there is still hope and that there is still goodness. I am trying to give back in my own way. I have every intention of doing my own Sparks in any way that I can to repay the kindness that has been bestowed upon me and my beautiful children. Have a wonderful, blessed day!

Best Night of Work Ever

"May the God of hope fill you with all joy and peace as you trust in him, so that you may overflow with hope by the power of the Holy Spirit."
Romans 15:13 (NIV)

I saw this today and thought of One Spark!

I am working late at night in a twenty-four-hour pharmacy. There are only three customers in the store: a scruffy but clean young couple and another gentleman. The woman in the young couple is very pregnant, and her partner is picking up a range of baby hats we carry and holding them up against her stomach, then looking at the prices and sadly putting them back. They pick up a packet of the cheapest pain medication we carry and bring it to the counter. Female customer: "I'm sorry, but can you please ask the pharmacist if these are safe for me to take?" Me: "Of course!"

While we are waiting for the pharmacist to come out, they tell me that they're expecting their baby girl any day now. The pharmacist has been watching the couple since they came in. Pharmacist: "These are fine, but can I ask why you need them?" Female customer: "Oh, I have a horrible cough that's making my back ache terribly. I can't even sleep." The pharmacist describes a list of cough medicines safe for her to take before the young man shakes his head. He has tears in his eyes. Male customer: "I'm sorry, I've just lost my job, and we really can't afford any of those. Sorry for wasting your time." Pharmacist: "That's okay, but this packet is damaged and, legally, I can't let you take it. Seeing as it is the last one, let me and Stacy go to the back room to look for some more."

The pharmacist and I walk into the stock room where, into a box, he places three packets of name-brand painkillers, four bottles of name-brand cough syrup, a wheat bag for her back, a tin of formula, a packet of newborn nappies, and a few of the hats the couple was interested in. He hands me the box and tells me to take it to them. I do and they both burst into tears, thanking us over and over again. They leave with huge smiles on their faces. Female customer: "Thank you again!" Other customer: "I'm sorry, I couldn't help but overhear. Did you say you just lost your job at a local company?" Male customer: "Yes, I was an IT tech." Other customer: "I own a computer store in the area, and I'm looking for a new technician. Can you start tomorrow?" There were tears all around that night. A week later, the young woman brought in her beautiful daughter and a giant batch of cupcakes for the pharmacy staff. Best night at work ever!

ELECTRIC COMPANY

"The King will answer and say to them, 'Truly I say to you, to the extent that you did it to one of these brothers of Mine, even the least of them, you did it to Me.'" Matthew 25:40 (NASB)

I wanted to share with you an amazing act of kindness that

was done for our family yesterday. Earlier, in July, our daughter had multiple brain surgeries, which left us playing catch up on a lot of our bills. Yesterday, I called one of our utility companies to let them know that we were going to be a day late making our payment. The account manager I spoke with became so excited when I called. It turns out that when we called in July to let them know we would be late on our payment (due to our daughter's hospital stay), the utility company started a donation fund for our family. Of course, we didn't even know this existed! She was so excited to tell me that we didn't need to pay our bill this month because it would just be taken out of the fund they had set up for us. I cried so hard I could barely choke out the words, thank you.

The utility company is planning on keeping the fund open to donations in case we run into more issues where we will be late or unable to pay. I was so moved by this random act of kindness that I have cried on and off since we were told about this. Very, very rarely are utility companies willing to go above and beyond to help those who need it most. The lady we spoke with said people are still donating to the fund, and they will only use it when we need help. God works in amazing ways. We felt so blessed that God had answered a huge prayer for our family. I am still in shock over it. I can't believe that this account manager has taken such an interest in our family that she took it upon herself to find a way to help us. She also gave us some great resources that will help out with other things. I feel like we have just given the Spark of a lifetime. Some day, some way, we will pay it forward.

MR. CALDWELL IN ARIZONA

"Keep your lives free from the love of money and be content with what you have, because God said, 'Never will I leave you; never will I forsake you.'" Hebrews 13:5 (NIV)
There is a man whom I've seen a couple of times around

Weatherford, Texas. He is old, disabled, homeless, and walks with two crutches and carries two carts. Today I was leaving the gym, and he caught my eye while he was walking up the hill on the access road. I decided to go to McDonald's and get him something to eat. I circled back and stopped to talk with him. He turned out to be the highlight of my day.

His name is John Caldwell. He served many years in the Air Force in Germany and France and was stationed in Alaska as well as a few other places. He is a traveler. He spends a lot of his time going back and forth between North Texas, El Paso, and Arizona. He said he calls Arizona "home." He likes the Weatherford region too. While he's in the area, he travels to North Texas truck stops that have laundromats, showers, and food. When I offered him the McDonald's meal, he first refused, saying he was heading to Whataburger and would buy something there. When I said I had already purchased a meal, he said he would "take it if I insisted."

When we spoke of his service to our country, I thanked him. He said, "I don't like to be thanked. I made the decision to serve and I was just doing my job." He continued with, "It's the teachers who deserve to be thanked." I offered to pay for a night in a nearby motel so that he could rest and enjoy a warm shower. He declined my offer. He said, "We only have a few more days of nice weather. When it's nice out, I prefer to be outside. If the weather were bad, I might accept your offer, but today I will pass."

John asked me if I knew of any preachers or Christians who would volunteer sometime by speaking and praying with the veterans at the Veterans Affairs hospitals. He said, "That's where the most help is needed." He further explained that the hospitals are usually short staffed in the chapel area and could use some extra people there. I told him I would gladly pass the word along and added that if I saw him around town again, I would stop and say hi. He simply said to me, "I'd appreciate that." I made sure he had enough cash for a night in a motel room if he needed it. He refused the money until I insisted. I asked if he had everything he needed or if I could get anything else for him, especially with bad weather coming. He patted his cart and said, "I have all I need. Thanks."

As I walked away, I began to cry. What a beautiful man this was. I don't know his whole story, but he wasn't looking for a handout or anything. He was humble and soft spoken. John Caldwell touched my heart today. I am giving him his "wish" and passing along his words. If you know anybody who is able and/or willing to donate some time at a VA Hospital, please let them know that their help is sorely needed. The veterans would probably enjoy a fresh face and a nice conversation—if nothing else. Tell them John sent you.

Children Understand – Disappointed Family Gives

"Train a child in the way he should go; even when he is old he will not depart from it." Proverbs 22:6 (ESV)

This past Christmas, my wife and I visited our old home town. There we learned of a young family with three children who had decided to forego their own Christmas presents in order to donate presents and food to a family in need. They all were quite disappointed to find out that they had to first give the presents and then that company would pass along the gifts to the other family. They were hoping to do it face to face so the three kids could experience the joy that their actions caused. Even so, it was the thought that counts. Unfortunately, this particular notion can be lost on a three- and five-year-old. They found themselves without any presents Christmas morning, but their parents said that their actions helped make another child extremely happy that day. I could tell that it was a difficult concept for them to grasp.

My wife and I decided to visit the local store and purchase whatever we could find that small boys might like. We took the gifts home, wrapped them, and delivered them to the children. When we showed up with the gifts, the kids were thrilled, but we made sure to impress upon them that this feeling is what their actions gave to the other family in need. Someone showed up at their door laden with gifts and put the same joy on their faces and in their hearts. The look of realization was plain on their faces, and it was obvious that they really understood. Being in this position—to not only pay it forward, but also to teach these children how important their actions were—priceless!

Their Miracle

"I am the Lord, the God of all mankind. Is anything too hard for me?"
Jeremiah 32:27 (NIV)

My parents are two of the most generous people on earth. They raised five children and gave us everything they could. A few years back, my father was laid off. He has had a hard time finding work ever since. But, my parents have not stopped giving. Two years ago, my mother and I were driving home on Christmas Eve when we noticed a dog and a young woman with a sign that read WE NEED A MIRACLE. Since it was minus zero degrees and snowing, we bought them food and hot chocolate. We really did not have much to give, but we could at least do that.

Soon after, the husband joined his wife, and they proceeded to tell us their story. They had walked to New York from Vermont because they were kicked out of their current housing. Their destination was upstate New York where they had family. They could not walk any farther because of the weather. Their clothes were torn and soaked, and they had a lot of blisters. We took their cell phone numbers, wished them well, and left—knowing we had no money to help them. We drove home.

It was Christmas Eve and this couple and their pooch were on our minds, so we got my dad involved. With his help, along with assistance from some other connections, we were able to rent the family a hotel room for almost two weeks—and luckily, one that took dogs! People brought them meals and Christmas gifts. Santa even visited them! A groomer cut the dog's nails. The couple received gift cards. In the end, transportation to upstate New York was provided for them to start their new life. This year on Christmas they called and said, "We have not forgotten your family."

Just Flip Flops

"and with your feet fitted with the readiness that comes from the gospel of peace." Ephesians 6:15 (NIV)

I was shopping with my mom and we were in the checkout line. There was a woman in front of us with a small girl, probably six years old. She was wearing a pair of dirty, broken flip flops that were too small for her feet. In her hand was a pair of new ones. Her mother went to pay and realized she didn't have enough money for their food and the flip flops. The little girl started to cry, saying how much the old flip flops hurt her feet. Very discreetly, my mom passed the cashier a ten-dollar bill. When they cashier bagged the flip flops, the mother and daughter realized what my mom had done. The mother was speechless and almost looked ashamed. My mom said to her, "Please don't worry. If I happened to be in your position, I'd hope that you would do the same." My mother is not rich by any means. She raised four kids on her own and managed to work and keep a well-balanced household. This one act of kindness shows you that anyone can help.

Need New Sweater

"John answered, 'Anyone who has two shirts should share with the one who has none, and anyone who has food should do the same.' " Luke 3:11 (NIV)

We live in an area where winters are normally not very cold or wet. In the span of only one week we experienced a freeze, temperatures down into the twenties, and rain. One morning that week my husband called me and told me that he needed a new work sweater, so I asked him why. He said he stopped at the Chevron and the usual homeless man was there, cold and trying to huddle in his cardboard. My husband took off his sweater, gave it to him, plus a few bucks for whatever he needed. He said that the man's eye teared up and managed to squeak out the words, "God bless." I have never been more proud of my husband; I feel blessed to have a man like that in my life.

Never Underestimate the Power of a Child's Love – Loving Others

"Above all, love each other deeply, because love covers a multitude of sins." 1 Peter 4:8 (NIV)

My story is very simple. It's one that saved my life.

I have always been a very positive, outgoing, friendly, caring individual. A few months ago I had a pretty dramatic encounter with my sister-in-law, who also was one of my very good friends. Long story short, there were hard feelings. We shared the same group of friends, and I was not surprised to see "my friends" and in-laws turn their backs on me after she filled them in on the whole ordeal. My family lives all over the county (except where I live), so needless to say, I felt more alone and vulnerable than I ever had in my life. I had my bunny and my cat to lean on and to cry to. I called my mom daily for two months straight, bawling because I felt so ridiculously unloved and unwanted by everyone here who still meant so much to me. All I wanted to do was fly to my parent's house and never see these people again. I wanted to run away from my problems, but since I couldn't, something very bad happened.

I turned into the person I promised myself I would never become. I felt defenseless, and as a result I became hateful, jealous, competitive, judgmental, and downright MEAN. I ended up hating myself more than I hated anyone or anything else. I constantly tore myself down, made snide remarks in my head, and convinced myself that I wasn't capable of love or being loved. I was a bitter, jealous, lonely woman—and I hated who I had become. To be honest, I was very close to giving up on life because I thought no one would care anyway.

Desperate to find some reason to stay on this earth, I drove six hours to see my sister and her kids. I was sitting with her family and thinking to myself, *What in the world am I doing here? I don't deserve to be around these people!* At that exact moment, my sweet five-year-old niece came over to me and gave me the biggest hug. She then stepped back, looked me in the eye, and stated, "I love you so very much Nikki. Thank you for coming to visit me. You are my friend, and I wish I could see you every day." It was almost as if God had prompted her at that precise moment to get through to me. Tears poured out of my eyes, and I sobbed as I embraced her for three full minutes.

Since that experience, I am still working very hard on loving myself again. I am making slow, but continual progress. I have found that I am able to love myself more by loving others. Although I am gradually building myself up and putting my relationships back together, I am grateful. Because of a five-year-old's hug and kind words, I am still here, and I am still trying.

Never underestimate the power of a child's love.

LIFE SAVED – PREGNANT GIRL WANTED TO COMMIT SUICIDE

"Give thanks to the God of gods. His love endures forever." Psalm 136:2 (NIV)

It has been a while since we last talked, and I have been reading the letters from people telling you what One Spark has done for them. I wanted to tell you and everyone that reads this why they should support One Spark. My school was the second school you spoke at with your "choices" speech.

The day you came to my school I had cut myself and had decided that I could no longer take this rotten life. Until I heard David's story,

I thought my home life was awful. His was worse! I thought, *This guy is only here for the money and really does not care about us.* Then, during his speech, Dave said that he did not charge anything. I listened to his words and thought, *Who is this guy and where did he come from?* As he continued to speak, I felt my heart start to soften, as tears began to flow down my cheeks.

You see, at fifteen I was carrying a very big burden and did not know how to handle it. I had been having sex and doing drugs for over three years and had just found out that I was pregnant. To make matters worse, I had parents who took drugs and drank every night. I was at the end of my rope and had decided that it was no longer worth the fight. Dave told many stories that day about kids and their situations. He told us about a girl like me who had become pregnant and tried to commit suicide. She was not successful, and they put her in a hospital to try to help her. She carried the baby for eight months and then committed suicide right next to a hospital. Because she was so close to giving birth, they were able to save her baby. Dave went on to say, "One day, that little girl is going to ask why she was not worth enough to her mother to keep fighting." Dave showed everyone a picture and said, "To this little girl, her mom would have meant the world to her." He went on to explain the pain that suicide causes—how horrible the situation is, as family and friends continually question what they could have done to prevent it.

When Dave finished his speech, I asked my teacher if I could speak with him for a minute. I went up to Dave and told him what was going on with me, including all the mistakes I had made and how rotten my life was. I can remember this, like it was yesterday, when Dave looked at me and said, "Your life is fine and this is nothing to worry about." We talked for thirty minutes, and he told me that he wanted to speak to both me and my parents later that night.

Dave showed up at my house, wearing his big smile. When he came inside, my dad was not being very nice. Dave looked him in the eye and said, "You should be ashamed of yourself." My dad quickly stood up and started to get mad when Dave said, "This is no longer about your wife or you; it's only about your daughter." Dave asked me to tell my parents what I was planning to do. When I told my parents that I was going to kill myself, they both began to cry. Dave stayed at my house until 3 AM and then headed back to his hotel. My parents and I stayed up all night talking about what all three of us needed to do to get clean for the baby. I can tell you, from that point on, we have not touched one drug. I have a six-year-old baby girl named Emma. She would not have been here without One Spark and Dave.

I would like to say a few words to teachers in schools who think Dave has a hidden agenda for coming to your school. You're right—he does—it's the kids. Some of you will say that he is there for the money, but when no money is paid out, you then say he is there to feed his ego. Well, you need to shut your mouth and realize that your negative comments could kill the very chance that someone needs in your school. If you have nothing better to do than complain about a program that does not cost you or your school a dime, then maybe you need to find a new line of work. Believe me—I have heard it all. What is he up to? Why does he do what he does? The bottom line is that there are four lives in my family whom he has changed. If not One Spark, then what program would you like to see that will produce the same results for the same amount of money?

Here is my request for everyone who can help this great program. I would like to see people committing to a specific dollar amount a month, like one or five dollars. This will help One Spark be able to predict what they will be able to do in the form of giving.

To everyone on this One Spark page, thank you for your help and the love of One Spark because it saved my life and my baby's.

Anchors to Keys

RAPED BY HER STEPDAD – NOW A COUNSELOR

"Forget the former things; do not dwell on the past. See, I am doing a new thing! Now it springs up; do you not perceive it? I am making a way in the wilderness and streams in the wasteland." Isaiah 43:18-19 (NIV)

Hi Dave,

I'm writing to tell you that you are my hero. I have read and re-read your story many times, and it has helped me get through one incredibly rough spot in my life. I am not sure if you remember me or not, but I am the girl who was being raped by her stepdad. My mother was so concerned with getting drugs, she didn't care that her husband was raping me. By the age of sixteen, I had one child by him and another was on the way.

Everyone in my school thought I was a loose girl. They didn't want anything to do with me. Well, that is not really true—most guys wanted in my pants because they knew someone else had already been there.

The reason I didn't run away and chose to stay in that horrible life was to protect my little sister, who was only ten years old. I would make sure to please him, so he would not want her. There were many times he threatened that he wanted her, but I could stop him by letting him do whatever he wanted to do with me—actions you can't imagine.

One day, I heard there was going to be a guest speaker at our school, and my counselor told me that I really needed to be at school to listen to him. I made sure that I was at school; I even pretended to be eager to hear this Spark guy. To be honest, in my life at that time, I really did not care that Dave was coming to my school, because I knew no one was going to be able to help me get out of my nightmare.

Dave began with his story of being sold and molested over 700 times. At that moment, my heart broke for him because I knew what it felt like to be used as a piece of meat for someone else's pleasure.

The more Dave spoke, the more I knew he was someone I could trust to help us get out of the rotten life we were living in. When he finished speaking, I almost ran to the front to talk to him. I waited in line for a little bit, and then it was my turn. I asked him if we could step away, and he said yes, but he wanted someone to come with us. So I asked my counselor if she would come with me to speak to Dave. She said yes. We went into a classroom that was not being used and that is when I told them both of them the life of misery I was living in.

After I finished telling them my story, I looked up and saw Dave and Karen were both crying. Karen said, "I'm going to have to report this." Dave asked me where my stepdad worked. I replied, "He works for the city." Dave and Karen decided to call a federal marshal one of them knew. About two hours later, the feds were in town, and my mother and stepdad were arrested. Later, both of them went to prison.

Dave and Karen reached out to my aunt who lived thirty miles away. I had not seen her since I was a baby because of the drugs that my mother was doing. She came to our town and picked up my sister and me and took us to her house.

For the first year of being away from my mother and her husband, I struggled with the question of why this had to happen to me, and that is when I called Dave. He said, "One day, your story is going to unlock the prison doors for so many women and young girls who have gone through what you went through."

This was twelve years ago. I am now married to a wonderful man and have three more children. He has adopted my first two, and no one knows they are not his children.

With the help from One Spark, I went to college and graduated. I went on to get my masters in psychology, and now I am a counselor at large school in a big city where I use my degree and experience to unlock the prison doors of many children.

Dave and I did not decide to be raped or to endure a life of a life of heartache, but through the grace of God, we have both turned our anchors into keys.

An anchor is a heartache that holds people in a moment of time, where something bad has happened to them, like being raped. I had a choice to stay really mad at my mother and her husband, but by doing that I was glorifying the devil—and he was winning. When I realized, with the help of Dave, that I now knew someone who had already been through something like I was going through, I could turn my anchors into keys and then glorify God.

In our actions and attitudes, we are either glorifying Satan or we are glorifying God! There is something else that happens when you refuse to anchor down after a bad situation or someone does you wrong. You take the power away from them when you forgive them and turn tragedy into a blessing for someone else.

Dave, I want you to know that my family loves you and what you have taught me. I am sharing with others to unlock their prison doors. God never seeks revenge, so I thought, *Why should I want revenge, when God never wanted it from me?*

I hope if you are struggling with something in your past, you will turn it into a key.

I am a true convert.

Passed Over For Principal – 27,000 Sparks

"Get rid of all bitterness, rage and anger, brawling and slander, along with every form of malice." Ephesians 4:31 (NIV)

Hi, One Spark.

I am seventy-one years young and have never loved life more than I do now. But that has not always been the case. For over fifty years I was a teacher, and I was a pretty good one. I was married for forty-five years to the best woman God could have ever given me. She put up with so much from me in our marriage. Surprisingly, she never left me.

I became bitter after I was passed over to be the assistant principal at our school that I had worked at for over thirty-five years. They told me that times were changing and they were not sure that I could embrace the new technology that we were going to be placed under in the future. I told them that technology was one of the biggest problems that schools and other entities were facing today because people have forgotten how to communicate.

I told the board that I have witnessed kids sitting next to each other and not saying a word to each other, but they were texting. Long story short, I was passed over for the position, and they hired a real dipstick.

Feeling sorry for myself, I started to drink heavily and became so angry that I could not see straight. Determined to show them, I made it my mission to throw a wrench into everything they were trying to do. As I look back now, it did nothing to the board or principal, it only hurt the kids I taught.

My wife became sick and went downhill very fast. Before I knew it, she was gone. This made me angrier and I was ready to through in the towel. I was determined to quit my job and move away from the town I had lived in all of my life. My resignation was written, and I had planned to hand it in on Friday. When I went into the office, the principal told me that we had a speaker that day and he needed me to help with the kids. What I really wanted to tell him was to shove it where the light did not shine, but I kept my mouth shut and headed to the gym to set up for the speaker.

When I arrived at the gym, there were several people setting up to speak to the kids. They had ducks set out, and this guy was in shorts walking around trying to make sure everything was ready for the speaker. I asked him when the speaker was due to arrive and he smiled and said, "Thirty-one minutes ago." Confused, I asked the young man where I might find the speaker and he told me I was talking to him. I was beside myself, and I know that he knew how I felt. So, I asked the guy why he was wearing shorts, and he said, "I don't look good naked." Trying not to laugh, the ice was broken, and we hit it off.

The speaker asked me to tell him a little about myself. I gave him the whole nine yards and even some more that I was sure he did not want to hear—like how I was cheated out of my position as the assistant principal and how my wife died. He smiled and told me to wait until he spoke, because he was sure my questions would be answered.

Immediately upon his stepping onto that stage, I could feel his compassion for the kids. I could even feel his pain from all the bad things that had happened to him as a child. I listened to him talk about anchors and keys and thought, *You have no keys to offer, and you are nothing more than a drunk.* Dave finished his presentation, I asked if he had time to meet after school, and he said yes.

I had so many questions for him. "How could you forgive the person who had done all the bad things to you? What caused you to move forward in life and leave the heartaches behind?" Dave and I talked for hours, and when we finished, I knew what I needed to do to get myself back on track in life.

I drove to my wife's grave and asked her to forgive me. Then I visited the principal, students, and other staff to ask them to forgive me for my attitude and how I had acted over the last few years.

From there my mission was to change the world I lived in, one Spark at a time. First, I offered free tutoring, and then I started to find out who was hurting or who needed something, and I would Spark them. I started the One Spark Club at our school, and now we have sixty-seven children who show up and want to make a difference in the lives of people around them.

I can see this is a simple concept that very few people really comprehend or even fully understand. Being kind is the greatest gift we can offer another human being. It is a gift that has the power to heal a broken heart, give hope to the hopeless, and even give someone the power to change their world.

I am just one man who has shown many people the importance of Sparking. In fact, combining my own Sparks with those of these other caring folks, the total comes to over 27,000 Sparks. You do the math. If only half of the people pass on a Spark, how many people have been impacted by the efforts of one?

Before meeting Dave, I used to think that one person had very little power to change the world, but today I stand corrected.

Committed Suicide When Kids Not His

"Consider it pure joy, my brothers and sisters whenever you face trials of many kinds, because you know that the testing of your faith produces perseverance. Let perseverance finish its work so that you may be mature and complete, not lacking anything." James 1:2–4 (NIV)

Heartache and Joy

I'm writing to tell you a story of heartache and joy from one of my friends. He was not only a friend of mine; he was a business partner as well. I had known him most of my life.

He was always full of joy, love, and kindness. While in college he met and later married the girl of his dreams. It always appeared to me that he was more in love with her than she was in love with him. I felt in my heart that she knew one day he would be successful and she had placed all of her chips on him.

Shortly after college we went our separate ways but always stayed in touch. Later, we started a business together. I had also accepted a job with another company where I was working full time. My job with the business was to be the money guy, and he ran the day-to-day operations. In spite of all of our dumb decisions, the company flourished and began to make a lot of money. That is when I really began to notice that his wife loved money more than she actually loved him.

She got ahold of the company credit card and racked up over thirty thousand dollars in charges. I was going to prosecute her, but he begged me not to because they had their first child on the way. Not long after that child, numbers two and three were born.

She made frequent trips to her old college town and always had a reason to stay a few extra days. Something deep inside of me knew that she was up to no good, but I could never prove it. Then one day a bombshell was dropped in our laps. His middle daughter was diagnosed with leukemia and needed a bone marrow transplant.

We both were tested to see if we were a match for her, and the strangest thing happened when the test results came back. The doctor told both of us that it was not uncommon for a stepfather not to be a good match. My friend looked at the doctor and said, "That doesn't make any sense because I'm her father, not her stepfather." The doctor replied, "The DNA results conclusively show that you are not her father."

He asked the doctor not to say anything to his wife, and we got up and went outside. He began to cry uncontrollably, looked me in the eye, and asked, "What in the world did I do to deserve something like this?" I hurt for him, not only because he was my friend and business partner—he was my brother.

We set a plan in motion to test the other two children to see if my brother was their father. In the meantime, I hired a private detective to start checking her out to see if there was anything she was doing that would explain this. Three weeks later the test results of the other two children came back. These kids were definitely not his either. My brother prided himself on being the world's best father, and in a matter of only one month he felt as though everything had been taken from him.

Our business was doing better than ever before, and three months later he asked if I would transfer his life insurance policies into his children's names. He also asked that I transfer all of the company stock into my name and made me promise that I would divide their profits up and place them into their trust accounts each year.

The private detective discovered that she had never stopped seeing the guy she dated before marrying my brother. After further investigation we found that all three children were fathered by her boyfriend. They had been having an affair ever since my brother married her.

We met for dinner one night, and again he asked me to make sure, no matter what happened to him, that his children would be taken care of. The next morning we were to meet at the gym, and he no-showed me. After no response, and not hearing from him for over three hours, I became concerned and frantically began to look for him. I pulled into a rental property that we owned together and found his rental car there. When I went inside, I yelled for him, but got no response.

I entered the house, and when I walked into the master closet, I found my brother had shot himself in the head inside of a box covered with sheets. He left me a note that read, *I'm sorry to do this to you a second time (our father had also committed suicide), but I could no longer bear living with a woman who had broken my trust and knowing the fact that I was not the father of those three children.*

When I called his wife to tell her what had happened, it was as though she didn't care. The only thing that she could ask me was where he kept his life insurance policies. I hung up the phone and didn't talk to her again until the funeral.

My brother had just raised his life insurance policies to make sure his children and their children would be taken care of. His oldest child was almost thirteen years old, and we were the best of friends. I spoke to her on a daily basis until the will was read and her mother found out there was nothing left to her mother.

Her mother became enraged and walked over to me as if she was about hit me. I said, "That would be the worst mistake of your life." She hired an attorney to sue the estate, and the judge quickly shot it down.

We transferred all of the life insurance proceeds into three trust accounts managed by a company with over a trillion dollars in assets under management. She continued to attempt to sue until the company became very aggressive and sued her. She then turned her sights on our company, trying to get everything she could from it, but that did not work either.

She then withheld the children from me and would not let me see them anymore. I would watch them from a distance to make sure that they were okay. Somehow, my nieces found out what their mother had done to drive their father to commit suicide. As an observer from the outside, it appeared to me that they just tolerated their mother until they reached age eighteen.

Each child could draw from their trust funds to go to college and to get a car, but they could not touch the rest of the funds until the age of twenty-four. It is amazing how time flies, because each of these children are now above twenty-four years old and have grown into fine young women. I speak to each of them on a regular basis, but I want to brag for just a minute on how great they have become.

The oldest has had a friend since she was two years old; they were thick as thieves and went everywhere together, even the bathroom. On her twenty-fifth birthday she called and said, "Uncle D., I have a question." She asked, "Do you think I should give one of my kidneys to my friend?" I told her that was not a decision that I could make for her; it was something she would have to decide on her own. She asked me, "If you needed a kidney, would my dad give you one?" I replied, "Yes, he would, and if I needed yet another kidney, he would give me his last one."

First let me explain how their trust funds work. They can only draw out of their trust fund exactly what they had earned the previous year. With that said, she not only gave her friend her kidney, she gave the amount she could draw out of her trust fund to give to her friend so she could continue to pay her bills.

The second daughter had a friend who had two children and was married. Her friend had cancer and had to take time off from work. She asked me if it would be okay if she gave her friend her money so that her friend would not suffer from the loss of her income during her recovery from stage four cancer.

His youngest daughter was always a handful and a free spirit. We frequently called her the tinman because we didn't believe some of the hurtful things she had done to her sisters. One day, she called and asked me to go to lunch. She said, "You know I have a boyfriend." I smiled and said, "That's great." She continued with saying, "He reminds me a lot of you. You often told me that you and my dad were like two peas in a pod, so I guess I found a guy just like my dad." She went on to say, "His life has been really rough. He's had to fight to make it where he is today." She asked me if it would be okay if they got married. I said, "I don't have to live with him, so it really is not my decision." She went on to say, "I'm not going to have the wedding of my dreams. Instead, I'd like to give my money to someone I know who needs it far more than me."

I knew in my heart I could not allow her to give her money away and not have the wedding of her dreams (or her father's dreams), so I asked her for her W-2s. I then gave her the exact amount that she had made the prior year as well precise amount she could draw from her trust fund.

I'm often asked what events I would choose as the greatest accomplishments of my life. I'd have to say there are two besides my own marriage: 1) walking two of my brother's children down the aisle; and 2) giving them away to their husbands.

I sat down with the three girls about a year ago, and they told me they wanted to go see their mother and let her know that they had forgiven her for what she did to their father. They had not spoken for quite some time because their mother was in prison.

From the time they were eighteen years old, each of them made the decision to follow the example their father had set for them by living a life filled with love, compassion, and kindness. We often talked about their father and the great gifts that he had, and they would always ask me what his best attributes were. My response was and is always this, "He was the greatest giver that I had ever known." My nieces chose to turn their anchors into keys and become blessings to their friends, family, and casual acquaintances. My brother and best friend's legacy will continue on through his three daughters.

LETTER TO DADDY!

"Behold, I am with you and will keep you wherever you go...."
Genesis 28:15 (ESV)

Hi Dave, One Spark, and everyone who is on this page.

I want to tell you about a challenge that was given to me in 1999. I was a senior in high school and loving life. I was ready to go to college and be on my own.

We had a guest speaker at my high school, and I had no clue what he was going to discuss. He started by talking about his childhood, and his story broke my heart. When he finished his speech, he gave everyone who could hear his voice a challenge. He asked us to do ten Sparks, and the first ones needed to start at home.

Dave asked us if our parents charged us for living in their home or for doing all the things they do for us, and everyone in the gym that day had to say no. Then Dave asked each one of us to write a letter to our parents, telling them how much we loved them, and how much we appreciated everything they do for us. I really was so lucky to have the parents that I did, because they loved me, and I knew it.

My dad was an army man. Trying to hug him was like trying to hug a porcupine. He was always in control of his emotions, and I had never seen him cry. I got out my pen and paper and started writing my mother first. That letter was so easy to write because she always showed her emotions and let you know how much she loved you.

When I began writing my dad a letter, my emotions started to pour out. Before I knew it, I had written five pages, front and back, telling him how much I loved him and that he was my hero. I told him that I have always considered him to be my hero and would never want anyone to take his place. From there, I told him that he made me want to be a better person. I added that I loved him for so many reasons, especially for defending our country.

When I gave my parents their letters, my mom said, "Thank you!" and started to cry. My father never said a word. I was hurt and confused, because Dave told me that it would make a huge difference for my parents. He also said if it did not, he would give one hundred dollars to me and every other person who did not get a positive response.

I called Dave and told him that my dad did not react to his letter, and that he was being deployed within two weeks. He asked me to send him the letter that I gave to my dad. Dave called me and told me that my letter was the best letter he had ever read, and it made him cry. He said to me, "Please wait one more week, and if he does not say anything to you then, I will mail you a one hundred dollar check."

A week went by and—still—no word from my father. Dave sent me a check like he promised. He said, "Remember, we never should do anything just to get a response." He then told me about all the letters he had written over the years that also received no response. Dave told me that he loved me and that he knew my dad loved me too. My father never brought up the letter. Years went by, and I finally stopped thinking about it. I imagined that he did not know what to say to me, and that is where I left it in my mind.

My father was over in Iraq. My mother was notified that he was killed in the line of duty and his body was going to be shipped home. A friend of the family went over to bring his remains home, and as he was going through his belongings, he noticed the letter I had written him almost nineteen years earlier.

My father was a Command Sergeant Major, and many of his troops were coming to see our family friend. They told our friend that my father read my letter every day, and many days he would read it out loud to his troops. Many of my father's troops were telling him how they enjoyed hearing the letter, even after the thousandth time. They told our friend that when my father read my letter, he would start to cry. They added that he frequently told them that he needed to be a better man for his daughter—his only child.

When my father's belongings arrived home, I found a little box and opened it. There was the letter I had written so many years before. Behind it were both letters my father wrote to me and many other letters from his troops, thanking me for the inspiration and love I showed my father. Many people wrote to tell me that if they ever had a daughter, they would want her to be just like me. I cried for hours, and then I felt so bad for being angry at him for not saying anything about the letter. My father wrote over 126 pages of letters to me, pouring his heart out. He said how proud he was to be my dad and how he looked so forward to one day walking me down the aisle.

When I am having a bad day, I find myself going to the letters my father wrote me. When I read his wonderful words of love, they give me the strength to live and fight one more day!

On the day I finally did get married, it was hard without my father, but I had a great stand-in. Dave walked me down the aisle and gave me to my husband. He told me how proud of me he was and how he loved me. He told me that if God would have given him a daughter, he would have wanted her to be just like me.

Dave, you say you have no children of your own. Not true, my friend. You have thousands of children who love you and call you their dad. I am one of them. It is scary to think of what my life would have been without you, One Spark, and all the wonderful people you have on this page.

Thank you, One Spark and David!

P.S. Many people were blessed by the letter I wrote my father, and I am sure some will be blessed as they read these words today. Here is my challenge to everyone reading these words! Write a letter to your parents, spouse, kids, and people you love.

Writing a letter means picking up a pen and writing on paper. Put it into an envelope and either give it directly to that person or mail it to them. **Do not worry about the response. Do it because it is the right thing to do!**

Pops, Ford, Wife, Cancer

"Many women do noble things, but you surpass them all." Proverbs 31:29 (NIV)

Hello Dave and the One Spark gang.

My name is Gus and I am seventy-five-years young. I have had a great life. I was married for fifty-five years to the best gal a man could ever ask for, much less deserve.

Although I have been on the One Spark page for over nine years, I've never felt the urge to send in my Sparks, because I was raised not to brag. Then one day I thought, *How in the world am I going to brag, if Dave does not put my name on the old Spark?*

So, to get to the Sparks we did, I have to tell you about my gal, Virginia. I met her when I was sixteen, and it took a bit to convince her she really needed to marry me. I told her that I was going to be a huge success, and she did not want to miss out on the ride.

She really did not want me or any of my silliness, so I had to step it up a notch to show her how serious I was about being a successful man. I found a job at a Ford dealership, washing cars. One day, a salesman did not show up because he drank too much hooch the night before. We were having a big sale. The sales manager said to me, "Get out there and sell some cars!" And sell cars I did. I sold so many cars, that the other old salesmen farts wanted me fired. The sales manager told them no.

I kept on selling cars, like candy to kids, and saving my money so I could get my best girl to marry me. Finally, she gave in and married me. She was seventeen and I was eighteen.

I continued to sell and sell and sell, and I saved my money like it was going to be my last dime. At the age of twenty, I found out about a Ford dealership that was for sale, a ways away from my home town. Virginia and I went there and asked the man why he was selling the dealership. He said, "No one wants to buy cars. I'm going to do something that makes more money."

I asked him how much he wanted for the dealership. The amount floored me, because I did not have near that much money saved. I hatched a plan with my bride to head up to Ford Corporate and get them to loan me the money. I walked into the corporate office where a woman asked me what I wanted. I said, "I'm here to get a loan to buy the Ford dealership in this town." She replied, "We don't give loans." I told her I really needed a loan so that I could purchase the dealership as well as support the three babies my wife and I had on the way. She looked at my wife and asked, "Are you really going to have triplets?" Virginia looked her right in the eye, lied her bottom off, and answered, "Yes I am." The lady then introduced us to the vice president of sales. I knew if I could get him to sit down for ten minutes, I could sell him—and sell him we did.

My bride and I went on to own seven dealerships; we certainly sold a lot of cars! She did give birth to three daughters—no, not at one time, you goof—one right after another.

Life was great, we were getting older, and our daughters and their husbands were running the stores. Then, the nasty cancer got my wife—and it got her bad. I think that cancer thought it had her and was going to put her in the grave. That would not happen. She was cancer free and loving life once again.

We were in our sixties when cancer came back to visit my wife again. It seemed as if he had brought a few of his friends to attack Virginia—in several areas. When our granddaughter asked us to visit her school to hear this Spark Giver speak, I said, "What in the world is a Spark Giver—a person that farts and then lights a match?" That is when my pretty bride said to me, "That will be enough." I have to admit it, when my wife said to do something, I did it. She was the only person on this earth I feared.

We went to hear the speech, and this crazy man came out in flip flops, shorts, and a t-shirt. I was not going to listen to this nut because of the way he was dressed. Who in their right mind would listen to a man looking like this? Every person in that building is who. I was amazed at how he had everyone's complete attention—even mine.

To make a long story short, Virginia and I were hooked on this Sparking thing and wanted to give it a go. Remember that she was still full of cancer, so what better place to start the Sparking, than in the hospital? We took everyone in that hospital a gift. They were so many happy people. We did more and more Sparks. I noticed that when my wife did them, she felt better.

I forgot to tell you that the doctors said Virginia had only five months to live. Well, she made it eleven more years before that stupid cancer finally got her. Before it did, my wife sowed love everywhere she went with the One Spark cards. She would often say, "Let's buy this," or "Let's do that," and I would be there to hand out the One

Spark cards. I said to the recipients, "This woman, who is dying, asked me to give this to you, and she wanted you to promise to pass a Spark on." Who could say no to a dying woman?

Dave, thank you for the call and for the visit. You made my wife so happy, and she wanted to remind you that she wished she was your mom, because she would have loved you so much. Virginia passed away three weeks ago, and it has been so hard. I have to say that this Sparking is the only thing keeping me going.

I told my kids that I wanted to give away every dime their mother and I had in the bank, because they are set for life. They all said, "That's a great idea, dad."

One Spark, you are the best thing in the world. If more people would get off their butts and be Spark Givers, the world would be a better place. So take it from this old man—your Sparks matter and they will change the world.

I have one last thing to say. If you do not like one thing that Dave and his pals at the Spark headquarters do, don't get you knickers in a knot—just look at all the great things they are doing. If you must leave, because you really don't like it, zip your lip and just leave. Don't sit around and spew hate about the only thing you don't like that they do.

I was always taught that if you don't like something, try to change it. I know a way we all could change One Spark—send a truckload of money to them. Listen, even one dollar would make a difference, but fifty dollars sure would be better.

Love, Pops.

From Jail to Working for Mary

"Therefore, if anyone is in Christ, the new creation has come: The old has gone, the new is here." 2 Corinthians 5:17 (NIV)
Hi, One Spark.

Often I would come to the One Spark Facebook page to see what everyone else was posting, because my life was out of control. It seemed no matter what I tried to do, it all just turned into one big mess again!

Most of my problems in life stem from poor choices. I've been making bad choices ever since I was thirteen years old when I rebelled against what my parents wanted me to do! In my mind they were trying to control me. Now, at the age of forty-two, I look back and see that they were only concerned for my well-being and were acting out of pure love.

For over twenty years of my life, I spent quite a bit of time in jail because of drugs, violent behavior, and armed robbery. After being out for a while, I had all but given up on life and was determined that I was ready to go back to jail.

One day I was standing outside of a grocery store begging for food and money, in order to be able to get by for the next couple of days. A lady in her seventies stopped me and asked, "Why in the world are you begging for food when there are so many jobs out there?" I looked her square in the eye and asked her, "Who would ever hire an ex-con?" She told me that her husband would definitely hire me if I was not on drugs and would not steal them blind. I asked her what type of work I would be doing, and this is when she looked me in the eyes and asked, "Does it really matter?"

Stunned at first, I sat there with a blank look and then realized that she was right. I needed a job really bad, and it didn't matter what they would have me doing, as long as I was getting paid! That is when this lady told me to be at their business the next day at 8 AM sharp! She asked me if I understood what sharp meant, and I answered, "Yes, I understand, and I promise to be on time." Then she said, "If you're on time, you are late."

The next morning I was going to show this old lady that I understood what being on time meant, so I arrived at 7:01 AM. To my surprise, when I got there, she was standing at the entrance with a huge smile on her face. She said, "I'm sorry you're late!" I asked,

"How can I be late when I'm fifty-nine minutes early?" She answered, "You're only early when you beat me to work." I knew that I was had, so I followed her inside to see what kind of job was waiting for me. Mary was this woman's name, and she told me that I needed to go down to the cafeteria and get me something good to eat. I said that I wasn't hungry, and she politely said, "Get your butt down there and eat something, before I give you a flogging!" Not wanting to argue with Mary since it was my first day, I went to the cafeteria knowing that I had no money to pay for food. As I walked in the cafeteria, a man told me to get in line and tell the cooks what I wanted to eat. I leaned in and said to him "I don't have any money to pay for food." He said, "That's great, because we do not take money, just love."

After breakfast I was ushered out to the shop where I met a lady who started to show me the tasks I would be performing. I could not believe how nice, patient, and kind Helen was to me. Every time I made a mistake, Helen would just smile, tell me it was all right, and then give me a big hug. I was thoroughly confused about what was going on with all these kind people.

The morning went by fast, and the next thing I knew it was 11:30 AM. Helen told me it was time to get to the cafeteria, and we did not want to be late. I told Helen that I did not have any money to pay for lunch, and she replied, "Baby that's okay; you can't pay with money here my friend, only love."

As I was sitting at lunch talking to Mary and Helen, I looked around and I saw a few people who had been on the streets with me. So I asked Mary, "When did you find those guys?" She told me that they go out looking for people every night who they can employ. I asked her if it was hard to run a business with a bunch of misfits. Mary looked me square in the eyes and told me, "There are no misfits in this building, son." I apologized, and she said, "Don't worry about it."

I've now been working at this company for ten years. Mary still comes in to work every day. She is eighty-years-young and can still outwork all of us. One day I asked Mary why she would start a company like this. She told me it was to give back to her community, her state, and the world for all the kind things she had experienced throughout her life.

Mary told me about a brief encounter she had with the young man who sparked her interest in giving. He told her that giving could and would change the world. He relayed to her his story that was full of heartache and despair. Mary told me that it was like the young man had climbed right out of the abyss and rose to the gates of heaven, and he was bent on changing the world, one Spark at a time. I asked Mary if she ever talked to the young man again, she told me no, and then she told me yes. She said that she's never had a verbal conversation with him since that day, but she reads about what he's doing on a daily basis.

I want to brag on Mary for little bit. Over the last seventeen years, Mary has employed more than 3,000 people, and 95 percent of them have come off the streets. Mary's husband died when she was fifty years old, and he left Mary enough money to live twenty lifetimes. After Mary's brief encounter with this young man, she decided to open a company and compete in an industry that was very competitive. We have not only competed but we have thrived in the arena we are in.

I now take 25 percent of everything that I earn and give it to the people who are my friends and still living on the streets. I have not figured out how people who are given so much from so many people refuse to pass on a Spark, just like they have been given.

The company now is set up in a family trust, so that it will go on for generations to come. It is not designed to make a profit, but to reinvest everything back into the business and into its employees. This is why Mary provides breakfast and lunch to all the employees for free.

ACT THAT HAS BEEN AN UNFORGIVEABLE FORGIVEN

"For if you forgive other people when they sin against you, your heavenly Father will also forgive you." Matthew 6:14 (NIV)

Good morning, Dave and One Spark.

I've been on your One Spark page for many, many years now, and it has been one of the greatest blessings for me to read other people's Sparks and acts of forgiveness, because I have been anchored down since 1993. That was the day that a gunman came into our small town church and killed four people. I lost my husband and my only daughter that day.

I prayed every day that God would make the man who killed my family suffer. There was not a day that I did not think about this man and the horrible acts that he committed against my family. Frankly, I walked away from God because I felt like God let me down in my greatest time of need.

I blamed God for what had happened to my family. I was in church with them, worshiping Him when this happened. I felt that if I was in church, God should take care of me and not allow anything bad to happen to anyone. When in reality, that is not how things work in life.

One day when I came across One Spark and began to read the Sparks of other people, I came across a woman who had lost her husband and her daughter in an automobile accident. The drunk driver who killed them was only seventeen. I told myself there'd be no way I would ever forgive this man for what he had done. Then I read the rest of the story. This young man was just a boy. Again, he was only seventeen. He had lost his father in the war, and his mother passed away of cancer. He had never had a drink until that night, but the pain became so unbearable, he tried to drown it with alcohol.

The truly amazing part of this story was when this mother and her parents went to the jail to visit the young man to tell him that she had forgiven him. And then, when he was released from prison, she provided and cared for him the best she could.

This was the beginning of my healing process, because I knew in my heart if this woman could forgive this young man for killing her daughter and her husband, I had to find it within my heart to forgive the man who killed my daughter and my husband.

Each one of you on this One Speak page have played a huge part in my recovery from the darkness—the darkness of hate, bitterness, loneliness, anger, and many more emotions I had never really felt in my life before this tragedy. I was raised in a great Christian home and knew right from wrong. I knew that I should forgive this man. It wasn't until I read the story mentioned above, and read every comment that was posted under the story, that I began to move.

Early one morning when I woke up, I asked God to forgive me of my sins of hate and anger. I asked God to open the door to go see the man who killed my family. I did not think that he would want to see me, for fear of what I might say to him. The request was sent to him and he accepted.

I arrived at the prison on the appointed day and time for our meeting. Before I went in, I sat in my car and prayed for God to relieve me of the anchor that held me back for so many years. Then I walked into the prison and sat down in front of the man who had killed my family. I said to him, "I bet you are wondering why I'm here," and he said, "Yes ma'am I am." I looked him straight in his eyes and said, "I forgive you for what you did to my family." I also told him that he needed to make amends with God and ask God to forgive him for the terrible things that he had done to the families of that small church.

He sat there quietly for what seemed like an eternity, but it was really only about thirty seconds. Then he looked up at me, with tears streaming down his face, and told me he was truly sorry for what he did. I listened to him for over twenty-five minutes, and not one time did he make excuses for his actions. Rather, he took full responsibility for what he did. He told me that he often thinks about committing suicide, and I told him that that would be the worst thing that he could do. He told me that he would have the rest of his life to rot in jail, and I asked him if he had thought about trying to help other people while he is in prison.

He sat there for a minute and then asked me to clarify what I meant. I told him that just because he asked God for forgiveness, that didn't mean he would ever get out of prison. I told him that God would forgive him the very second he asked for forgiveness, and then he would give him a mission. I suggested that he lead a Bible study in order to teach young men how to make it on the outside when they get out of prison. I added, "I don't really know what God has in store for you, so you need to pray and ask God for guidance."

As I was about leave, I asked the guard if I could give him a hug, and the guard looked stunned and then said, "Yes." I gave this man a hug, told him that I loved him, and said that he would be in my prayers every day. The man was crying as he said, "Thank you." As I turned to walk out of the meeting room, I noticed five or six other people crying—the guard was one of them.

I believe that day many people's lives were touched by God through the compassion and grace that God put in my heart to bestow on that man. I later received a letter from the guard that said that my active compassion, love, and grace led him to understand that there truly was a God and he accepted Christ as his personal Lord and Savior.

I have since remarried, and at the age of forty-five, I am due in one month to deliver twins. I believe God has honored my willingness to forgive, and he has blessed me with not one child but two.

David, you're right about anchors and how they can destroy your life if you do not deal with them. The sad thing about my life is the number of years I lost because it took me so long to deal with the anchors that were holding me captive and would not let me move forward to serve God or to live a productive life.

My prayer is that if you are reading these words, you will please search your heart and find the people and/or situations that have caused you hurt (that have become anchors in your lives), and ask God to remove them and forgive the people who have wronged you—because it is only when you forgive yourself and other people that God can begin to move and operate within your life.

When you let go of the hurts that have paralyzed you with hate, anger, misery, unforgiveness, and many other emotions, your life will become filled with emotions and love from Christ Jesus.

A Life Changed

Dear One Spark.

I wanted to share the Sparks that were given to me about five years ago. I never knew what a Spark was until the person who helped me gave me a One Spark card.

I come from a very good family with two loving parents. We lived in a nice house and never had to worry about going without. Through a series of poor choices, I landed in jail for over ten years of my life.

Once I was released from jail, I had to find a job. It is not easy for a felon to find employment in the first place, but when you add in that my crimes were aggravated, it makes it even tougher. I had been looking for what seemed to be weeks upon weeks, and everyone told me that they would give me a call back—but never did.

One day while I was sitting in a park, several trucks pulled up. I could smell the delicious food cooking. There was a man, his wife, and their children tending to one of the grills—Dave and the One Spark foundation folks on another. One of the guys who regularly dined with Dave told me that all the food they give out is free, with one exception—diners had to give them a hug in order to eat. I told him that I would not hug anybody, not even the Grand Poppa of the One Spark Foundation. Then a homeless guy said to me, "I bet you will, if you want to eat."

I walked up, got in line, and noticed that everyone there was getting a hug. When it came my turn, I stuck out my hand and told Dave, "I do not give men hugs!" He looked me in my eyes and said,

"I'm so sorry you do not believe in hugs, because now you are not going to be able to eat the food we have prepared for you today." I reluctantly did what he asked of me because I was starving. When the man started to hug me, I did not want to let go, because this was the first hug that I had experienced in over twelve years.

He said that he loved me and then added, "Get on up there and get some good food!" I chose a hamburger with all the trimmings, chips, cookies, two or three side dishes, and dessert. I felt like I had just won the lottery. I definitely was not used to eating such high quality food that had been prepared with love.

I began to talk to Dave and another fellow named Brad. Both of them were funny guys, but Brad said something to me that I've never forgotten. He said, "I've always been a huge jerk, but coming out here and serving people like you really started to change me." Brad gave me a hug, and I could tell that was something he was not used to doing.

I asked Dave if he knew anybody who was hiring, and he said, "Yes, one of my companies actually is looking for employees." To make a long story short, I got on with Dave and worked with his company for two years. One day I told him that I really wanted to start my own business, so I was going to be leaving to pursue my new endeavor.

I've now owned my own business for over three years, and I am in a position to give back to my community by hiring recovering felons. They know that I'm not going to mess around with them, or put up with any of their rubbish. My landscape company now employs nine people. I truly believe that One Spark can start a fire in a heart that will never burn out.

Dave, I love you like my brother. You've taught me so much about life and about being a Spark Giver. I now take 15 percent of every dollar that I make and reinvest it into the homeless and needy.

I am urging every person who that reads this to take the time to also read all of the wonderful things One Spark is doing—lives are being changed. I will promise you that if it was not for Dave and One Spark, I would be back in prison. I am asking you to look into your heart and determine what amount you could afford to give this month and over the next twelve months as well.

I am a life that has been changed because of Dave, One Spark, and each person who has taken the time to post something on One Spark's Facebook page. Thank you to everyone who has made a donation. You have allowed Dave to help people like me get back on their feet.

In my two years of getting to work with one of Dave's companies, I've been able to see and experience what true love is really about. I look at the numbers on this page and realize that it would be a true blessing if each person would give one dollar, five dollars, twenty dollars, fifty dollars, or maybe even one hundred dollars per month to help One Spark change the world—one Spark at a time.

Loss of a Child

"You have turned for me my mourning into dancing; you have loosed my sackcloth and clothed me." Psalm 30:11 (ESV)

David and One Spark have made a huge difference in my life. David's story of heartache, anchors, and keys gave me the strength to finally change my anchor to a key.

My daughter was my whole life, and nothing fulfilled me more than being a mother. I felt I was created to be a mother, but I never planned on being a single mother. But life had a different plan for me. The guy who got me pregnant did not want to be a father, so he went on to college and I never saw him again. My daughter, Jane, has never met him.

Jane was a ball of fire and lived to play sports. As she got older, she found her stride as a pitcher on many softball teams. She was destined to go to college on a scholarship. As a junior, her high school team won the state championship; that summer she was going to play with her summer team.

My daughter turned sixteen and was living life to the fullest. Jane was also a good student who wanted to go to college to obtain a degree in law. She was so sweet. She told me that she was my retirement, and I had nothing to worry about when I got old.

One sunny day, my whole world changed when I received a phone call at work. It was from one of my daughter's friends who said that Jane was running to dive into the pool when she slipped and hit her head. Bleeding internally, she was non-responsive. I jumped up and told my boss I had to rush to the hospital.

When I arrived at the hospital, the doctors informed me that they needed permission to make an incision in her skull to help relieve the swelling that was putting pressure on her brain. I told them, "Yes."

The first twenty-four hours were horrible. Just as Jane seemed to be getting better, she took a turn for the worse. In only forty-eight hours, the doctors told me that they could no longer detect any brain waves.

They asked me what I wanted to do. I said, "Please give her a few more days." After five days, there was no change. I sat by her bed and told her that it was okay to go to heaven. There were four other family members in the room when I said that to her. She then smiled and squeezed my hand. I knew that it was time to let her go.

Jane passed away within minutes of taking her off all life support.

Sitting in her room with my mother, who had always been there for me, I lost it. I literally could not move. That is when my brother picked me up and helped me home.

Over the next few years, I found that I was drowning my pain in a bottle. I was so bad that I am surprised that my boss and owner of the business where I worked did not fire me. He was there for me even when I was not there for myself.

One day while I was surfing the web, I came across the One Spark Facebook page. Dave had posted his story on that particular day. I could not imagine how bad the pain must have been for him. I shot an email to One Spark, and Dave responded!

I told him how sorry I was for what he had been through, and he asked me to call him, so I did. We spoke for over three hours. He told me all about his heartaches and how he changed his anchors in life to keys. David said to me, "You need to do the same thing." He said that, even by his relaying to me his story of transformation, of a life full of anchors, he was turning his anchors into keys.

I remember him telling me he loved me, and then he told me to get to work on changing my anchors in life to keys—keys to release others from their anchors. I also told him that I loved him.

When I hung up the phone with Dave, I called my mother and asked her to come to my house. She was there in a flash. When she walked in, she was worried. I smiled and told her that I was okay and wanted her to help me get rid of all the alcohol in my home. I also told her that I was going to use Jane's story to change my anchor into a key. My mother looked at me funny, and I explained to her what I meant and how I found out about changing anchors to keys. I told her about Dave and One Spark. She started to cry, and told me that she was so happy I had decided to change, because this is what Jane would want me to do.

My key from Jane's death is to help parents who have lost children move past their pain, so they would never have to experience an anchor from the loss of their child.

Today I am now forty-one, married, and expecting a little girl. Yes, her middle name will be Jane—to carry on the life of her sister she never knew.

I urge each person who reads this to take a look in your heart and see if there are any heartaches that have a stronghold in your life. It may be someone who wronged you, cheated on you, left you, abused you, raped you, or something else.

Or, you may be the one that needs to ask for forgiveness in order to transform your anchor into a key. You have to be willing to let go of the hate, hurt, betrayal, disappointment, abandonment, and pride. If you don't, you will remain anchored in a miserable place.

In the last few years, I have used Jane's key to help over fifty families transform their anchors into keys. Now these families are they are using their keys to help others unlock their prison doors and change their heartaches into keys.

Love, your anchor killer.

What's Yo Pickle-Anchor

"But you must put them all away: anger, wrath, malice, slander, and obscene talk from your mouth." Colossians 3:8 (ESV)

I was in New York City for business when I realized I either had to take a cab or ride the subway to reach my destination. Both were scary feats for a boy from the rural Midwest. After watching the crazy cab drivers, I chose the lesser of two evils—the subway.

Once down in the black hole called the subway, I started to rethink my choice. Then I looked up and the train was in front of me. I mustered up my courage and bravely jumped on the subway. Once on, I wandered for a few feet and sat down next to a woman with whom I tried to strike a conversation. That went over like a turd in a punch bowl.

I continued to attempt to have a conversation with her and she continued to ignore me. So I decided she was going to hear me. That's when I looked over at her and asked, "Do you smell that?" She asked me, "Did I smell WHAT?" I said, "I farted." She asked, "You did what?!" And I told her, "I was just kidding. I really didn't fart." She looked like she had swallowed a skunk and her attitude smelled like one too.

Then I asked her, "What's your problem?" She snapped back, "Which one?" I said, "Whatever one has you anchored down." She said, "I don't know what in the world an anchor is." I told her what an anchor was and that I had many in my life that caused me to be mean and nasty, "just like you."

She looked me square in the eye and asked me, "What's yo pickle?" I told her, "It must be a dill." I don't think she understood the humor because she looked meaner and madder than a polecat. She said, "I don't understand who dill is, but I want to know what your pickle is." I said to her, "I'm not sure what a pickle is."

She then explained to me what a pickle was. We shared back and forth, and she told me what had happened to her as a child as well as what had happened to her in her first job in New York. At an early age, she was molested by her brother. Then, at the age of sixteen, she took a nanny job in New York, and the man of the house tried to rape her. She had also stolen three hundred dollars from her best friend, and this was a major pickle in her life.

I was so caught up in the conversation that I lost track of time. When I saw what time it was, we were standing in front of a shoe shine stand. I told her, "I just missed my flight to go home." That's when she said, "The reason you missed yo plane is because you ain't got yo pickle out." I said, "Mary, I don't know what pickle you are talking about. It kind of sounds bad." She looked at me and said, "I ain't got no time for your nonsense. You know what pickle I'm talking about."

We sat and talked about anchors and pickles for a few hours. Mary was a shoe shiner and she was one of the best shoe shiners I had ever seen—and I had a pair of shoes on that could prove it.

Mary had quite a few customers waiting in line to have their shoes shined. Suddenly, a man hopped up onto the stand and said to her, "You have to hurry. I have something important to do." Mary looked up and asked, "What's yo pickle?"

Mary continued to ask the man the same question and he continued to say to her, "I don't have time for this!" Mary replied, "You will not get your shoes shined until you tell me what your pickle is."

That's when I jumped in and explained that a pickle is something bad that has been done to you or something bad that you've done to someone else that still has a stronghold on you. I told him, "We call it an anchor where I come from." That's something that has you stuck and doesn't allow you to move forward to honor God with your life. I went on to tell him that our heartaches in life will either be a testament to Christ or they will glorify the devil.

Mary asked him again, "What is your pickle? He answered, "I

don't have one." That is when Mary told him to get up out of her chair. He said, "But I really need this shine!" Mary came back with, "You better come on with your pickle then." The man in a hurry then told her that he had cheated a business partner out of a lot of money, and that it had bothered him for many years. Mary told him that he needed to take care of his pickle before she would give him a shine again. He told Mary that he would make it right.

The next person in the chair was a woman, and Mary asked her what her pickle-anchor was. She answered, "I heard the conversation you had with the man before, and my pickle-anchor is that I was raped a few years back." Mary said, "Girl, I know what you mean, but I have to tell you that your pickle is not near as bad as this man's. He was molested over a hundred times and he found a way to turn his pickle-anchor into a key. I will let him tell you how that works for him."

I began to tell her that when we share our story, we use our story as a key, and that key has the power to unlock someone's prison door. I went on to tell her that many people live inside the prison of the heartache that happened to them. The woman said, "I'm going to turn my pickle-anchor into a key, starting right now."

The woman got up, and then Mary said, "Next…!" A little girl stepped up to Mary and said, "I know what you mean about a pickle-anchor." She told everyone standing there that she had been molested since she was four or five years old and that her stepdad was still molesting her now. Mary jumped on the phone and called some goon to go break the legs of the stepdad. She then asked the girl where her mother was. I asked Mary, "Why do you want to know where her mother is?" She told me that she was going to carve her like a pumpkin. Then Mary asked, "Girl, where you going to live?" The little girl answered, "With you."

You see, when Mary was molested as a young girl, there was so much damage done that she could never have a child of her own.

Mary said, "Child, you can't live with me because I live in a hole." The girl replied, "So do I." Mary said, "How am I going to afford to pay for you to go to college?" Just as that came out of her mouth, several people told Mary that they would help. Before the end of the day, Mary had enough money to send that girl to wherever she wanted to go to school.

There were so many people who went to bat for Mary to keep Baby J that soon she was living with Mary in a new apartment that was donated to her by the building owner (who was not known for his generosity).

Over the next several years, I would see Mary three to five times a year. Every time Mary asked me, "Boy, what is your pickle-anchor?" I shared with her what was going on in my life. Then I would ask Mary, "What is your pickle-anchor?" Mary told me that the only pickle-anchor left in her life was to find her friend who she had stolen money from all those years ago and repay her. Mary asked me if I could help her find her friend. I told her that I would try.

I jumped on the net and started to look for her friend. After a couple of weeks, I actually found her. I called her up and asked her if she knew Mary. She got rather pissed off and said, "That woman ruined my life, and I will never forgive her for what she did." I told her that Mary had asked me to get in touch with her and that she wanted her to come to New York, all expenses paid. I said, "Now you have a chance to get some of Mary's money." She laughed and said, "Well, I'm down for that!" I booked her flight and made her hotel arrangements.

I was going to be there for this reunion, and Mary promised that this was going to be a pickle-anchor breaking event. We picked up Mary's friend at the airport, and the conversation did not get off to a good start—Mary's friend was still mad about her stealing her money.

Mary told her that she was sorry, handed her an envelope, and told her to open it. Mary asked her to read the letter first, and she did. I looked in the rearview mirror. I could tell that the woman was crying, and then she looked into the envelope. I could see she was quite shocked. She said to Mary, "You really didn't have to do this." Mary replied, "Yes, I do because this has been a huge pickle-anchor in my life, and it has haunted me ever since the day I stole from you."

Mary never told me the reason she stole the money, but her friend let me read Mary's letter. In the letter Mary told her that she needed the money because her stepdad wanted to have his way with her and she knew if she stayed, she would have killed him.

Mary gave her friend the money she stole from her, plus interest—ten thousand dollars. The money was nice, but it was not what changed her friend that very day. It was that Mary took her friend's pickle-anchor away from her and gave her the peace she so needed.

Mary, her friend, Baby J, and I went to dinner that night. I was so touched by the love and kindness that was shown that day—it was as if these two friends had not missed the last twenty-four years.

Mary continued to put a mean shine on a pair of shoes and ask people what their pickle-anchor was. Baby J was doing very well in school—so well, in fact, that when she took her ACT, she got a perfect score. Baby J went to Harvard and received dual degrees in law and accounting. She is still doing well.

Mary continued putting perfect shines on shoes, right up to the day the Lord called her home.

I went to the funeral and when I walked into the place, I saw a huge anchor and an even bigger pickle. I was asked to speak at her funeral, and I asked everyone what their pickle-anchor was. The church was packed and people were telling all kinds of stories of Mary and her pickle-anchors. She would not give anyone a shoe shine until they told her what their pickle-anchor was in life.

I have not thought about this story much until today. As I type these words, I am choking back tears, because God blessed me with such a wonderful friend—I knew I could tell her anything.

I am sure that all the angels in heaven have a spit shine on their shoes.

Notes from the Author

Here is what I have learned through my many pickles. We were not born with a bag of Faith, Courage, Strength, or Resilience.

I have said from the start that I am a Christian, and I put my faith in Jesus Christ. This does not mean that you have to have the same faith that I do; it only means that you have to have faith in order to start the healing process.

It takes faith to muster up the courage to start moving forward. Any forward momentum is a positive thing because when we sit idly, that is when we begin to anchor down. That is when our problems start to fester and our lives become stuck.

Our lives will only change when we develop enough courage to change our lives and move into a better spot in life. Courage is like a muscle; the more we work at it, the stronger it will become. So the strength that has matured while working on our courage will rapidly effect change in our lives. As we develop our courage, we find renewed strength that will allow us to rewrite our pasts, move through life's storms, and arrive at a better place.

The continued advancement of our courage and strength will monumentally assist us when dealing with a pickle or a massive storm. It offers us resilience. Resilience is the ability to bounce back from one of life's pickles, or even a pickle that has gone bad and turned into a storm.

As I look back over my life, I have found that without these four components, I would have never been able to heal or to turn my pickles and anchors into keys. Combining my faith, courage, strength, and resilience allows me to tell my story (my key) to those who have gone through, or who are currently going through, what I've experienced in my life. I am able to insert my key into their hearts and unlock their prison doors.

Let me give you an example. I was molested many times, so when I talk to people who are struggling with the same experience, I can share my key (story) and help them heal their pickle. I have found that by sharing my key with people who have gone through what I've previously experienced, I can help them heal faster and give them a road map to healing.

Here is how this has worked for me. It's all about Faith, Courage, Strength, and Resilience. It seemed as though, once I gained a little faith, a bit of courage began to mount. But then I would fail and become frustrated. Subsequently, the fear would set in, and then I would have to head back to strengthen my faith. Many times I would be stuck there for a little while, before being able to muster up the courage to move forward. As my faith strengthened, I found I developed more courage. And just when it seemed as though my strength was building, I would fail again. (Failing means either I would not do what I wanted to do and I would do what I did not want to do, or I failed at a goal.) I might move back to working on my courage, or I might be back building my faith, which is really my 'why.'

I hope by now you see that I am always going back and forth between these momentum builders. I might be very resilient in one area of my life while still attempting to build my faith or my why in another area. In my life I've found, upon withstanding one storm, another one seems to be waiting around the next corner.

I'm not saying that everything will immediately turn out perfectly for you upon developing these four areas in the midst of your own storm. Be patient with yourself, because it probably will take some time.

I want to take a moment to speak to women who have found themselves in the middle of a storm called abuse. It does not matter if it is physical or mental. It is wrong, and the damage it causes will last a lifetime. My parents got divorced when I was a young boy, but years later I still am able to recall all the abuse my mother suffered. For countless years I witnessed these cruel treatments she withstood.

In reflecting upon her experiences, as well as my own childhood horrors, here is what I have learned. Many women choose to stay in abusive situations for the "sake of" their children. If they could only see the damage that this abuse has on their children, they would leave immediately. They would come to realize that some children don't have the strength to ever get over this pickle, and it will—for sure—turn into an anchor.

Women, you do not have to bear the abuse, and there will be life after leaving the abuser. I hope that one day you will understand that true beauty is on the inside and what is on the outside is just the pretty bow on the package. You deserve to be treated like a queen, and the only way that will ever happen is for you to demand it.

Sorry, I know it seems as though I have gotten off track, but I have not, because the abuse I witnessed my mother undergo still has a lasting impact on my life. Today, I use these memories and experiences as a key, but how wonderful it would be to never have had to develop that key in the first place.

I want to share a little insight as to what *to* say and *not* to say to people who are in the midst of a storm or fighting a pickle. Your friends or loved ones may be dealing with a death in the family, cancer, divorce, or some other type of deeply challenging life situation. When my father committed suicide, everyone asked me, "David, what can I do for you?" This simple, loving question actually put a lot of pressure on me. I knew they wanted me to give them an answer, but the sad fact was that I had no clue what they could do for me, let alone what I could do for myself.

Just let them know you love them, and that you will be there whenever they may need you. Give them a hug and then wait. You can drop them a text that says, "I am thinking of you and I love you." But, please do NOT ask them WHAT YOU CAN DO FOR THEM!

I think when people are in the middle of a storm, you need to offer them your ears to listen—please realize that they may not need a response from you—just listen. They may need you to be there, and it may be to just sit there and say nothing. What most people really need is your love and your willingness to be there when they need you. Your desired presence may not be required immediately—the request may arrive at 3 AM. More than likely it will not be convenient for you, but you need to stop what you are doing and willingly go to them.

Here is what I think you should do. Let them know that you are there for them, tell them you love them, and then give them a big hug. Then WAIT! If you do not hear from them, send them a text and let them know they are in your thoughts and prayers.

I think that more people will appreciate this when they are in their battle with a storm, than you continually asking them, "What can I do for you?"

I want each person reading this book to know that you are never alone and that you will always be loved. I promise that I will be there for you as much as I can. I will love you, and I want you to know that I am only one email away. My email address is dhill@1spark.net.

To the many people that I have hurt, wronged, or was mean to along the way, I am truly sorry, and I hope that you would forgive me.

Love, David A2J

STEPS I'VE USED TO TURN MY PICKLES AND ANCHORS INTO KEYS!

Honestly face and identify your pickles and anchors. This will allow you to deal with old wounds.

If you will deal with your pickles as they occur, and not bury them deep inside of you, they will never have a chance to turn into anchors.

An anchor is a pickle that was never dealt with and subsequently has a stronghold on your life.

1. Accept it!
2. Open up to the pains of your past. This is the only way you will be able to deal with them and move forward.
3. Grieve. This is a great thing to do; it will help you heal. Make sure that you do not grieve too long, or you will be stuck.
4. Get help! This could be from a friend or a professional. If you are opening up to someone, be very careful that they have your best interest at heart.
5. Be real where you are at right now.
6. Take control of your life.
7. **Forgive others and ask for forgiveness.**
8. Move forward. Start doing something to get better or to make a situation better.
9. Get vertical! My vertical is through God. Yours might be a higher power or something else.
10. Move from an internal thinker (all about me and my situation) to an external thinker (putting others' needs and wants before ours).
11. Learn to be a giver. The best life we could ever hope to live will be lived while serving others.
12. Develop an attitude of Gratitude.
13. Realize that you are going to stumble along the way. You might slip back into the person you were before you started to change. Failing is not fatal; it is just one step closer to victory.
14. Turn your pickles and anchors into keys that will have the ability to unlock someone else's prison door. A key is your story. By sharing your story, you have the ability to turn it into a key. Your key can help someone else get through a pickle that you have already made it through, faster and with less work and pain, because they have the wisdom of your

pain. Your pain can be someone else's gain if you share your keys with other people!

Love, David A2J

P.S. What does A2J mean? ... Addicted to Jesus!

Acknowledgments

I thank God for being in my life and always being there to pick up my messes.

To my Granny Scott for showing me that I was loved, and that it had nothing to with if I was good or bad. Thank you for teaching me about God and showing me the power of prayer.

To my father for teaching me to be tough and how to be a Spark Giver. I only wish I would have seen your gift when you were alive.

To my mother for giving me peace the last few days you were alive and for showing me that you did love me.

My brother Tony, you are my rock. Every day I ask God to make my heart like your heart. You have taught me so much, and I love you more than all the fish in the sea. You are the best brother anyone could ever ask for, and I can only hope one day to be the brother to you that you are to me.

Josh Turner, I wanted to say thank you for showing me that I am not alone and that other people have pickles just like me. I get up every day inspired by who you are and what you do. You make me want to be a better person.

I want to thank Penny Wood for having such a strong belief in me, that she drove me to college and got me enrolled. Without you, there would be no me, and there would be nothing but a tragedy.

I want to thank my editor, Tracy Johnson, for her wonderful work and unbelievable patience and kindness throughout this process. Through this book she has become more than my editor; she has become a trusted friend who has tirelessly given to this project just like it was her very own. If you are looking for an editor, you should chose my editor, because she has a gift of making sense of words that don't seem to make any sense at all.

I want to thank everyone at Kingman High School who played a part in my life. You made me the person I am now. Without your love, I am 100 percent certain that I would have committed suicide.

To my friend Steve, you taught me what real love was. You taught me to be a friend, and I miss you every day. We were the odd couple, but you were the glue that held our friendship together. I know you are in heaven getting the angels to sing in a choir and praising God all day long.

I want to thank my mother's boyfriend, John, of almost thirty years, for all the love and support you gave my mother. You were her rock, and she loved you more than all the fish in the sea.

To everyone who has helped with the mission of the One Spark Foundation, I want to tell you that you are the reason that One Spark has already changed—and will continue to change—the world, one Spark at a time. Without our volunteers, there would be no foundation.

I want to thank each person who picks up this book in the hopes of finding the answers to their pickles and anchors. I promise you that if you turn them into keys, you will change not only your life, but the lives of people who are hurting just like you. Thank you, dear reader, for investing in the words of a crazy custodian and for passing on the lessons you learn in this book to those others dealing with heartache.

Remember that one Spark can change the world—the only unknown is if it will be your Spark that starts the fire in someone's heart.

There is nothing more powerful than love and kindness, and the One Spark Foundation was founded on the Scripture.

Matthew 22:34–40 New International Version (NIV)

The Greatest Commandment

[34] Hearing that Jesus had silenced the Sadducees, the Pharisees

got together. [35] One of them, an expert in the law, tested him with this question: [36] "Teacher, which is the greatest commandment in the Law?"

[37] Jesus replied: " 'Love the Lord your God with all your heart and with all your soul and with all your mind.'[a] [38] This is the first and greatest commandment. [39] And the second is like it: 'Love your neighbor as yourself.'[b] [40] All the Law and the Prophets hang on these two commandments."

If you are looking for a place to give, that will use your money only for the cause, then give to the One Spark Foundation! We could use your help in funding the mission of changing the world one Spark at a time.

Check out the One Spark Foundation at www.1spark.net

About the Author

Who is the frog with the most warts? Yep, that would be me. I do not have it all together and never will. I get up every morning with one simple mission: to leave the world a little better than when I found it. Many days I am sure that I fail, but I get up the next day and try to leave footprints of love on all the hearts of the people I meet.

I have been blessed in so many ways and more than I can say. I have not received the just punishment I deserve, and for that I am forever thankful to the Lord Jesus Christ for dying on the cross for me when I was a wretch—and really still am.

Grace and only grace can save me. If it were not for grace, I would surely spend eternity in the abyss.

I am silly enough to believe that kindness and love can heal a broken heart, mend a broken relationship, and give hope to the hopeless. I believe that if you and I combine our Sparks with everyone else's Sparks, one day they will turn into an inferno of love that no one will be able to put out!

The only unknown here is if you will be willing to put your Sparks in to help start an inferno of love that could never be put out.

If you need someone to talk to, send me an email to <u>dhill@1spark.</u> <u>net</u> and I will get back to you ASAP!

Love, David A2J

Here is my challenge for every person that has read this book.

1. As I have said before and will say again, to be a true Spark giver, it has to start at home. Write a letter to your spouse, mom or dad, your children, and/or significant other. Let them know how much they mean to you and how much you love them.

   Writing means to pick up a pen, paper, and an envelope and write the letter. Then put it in the thing called an envelope and mail it or give it to them.

2. Write a letter to someone that has encouraged you to become who you are or who is loving where you are at, until you get to where you want to be.

3. Then I need you to write a letter to someone you know that could use a bit of encouragement.

   Next, write down how this made you feel and how you think it made the person receiving your letter feel.

   A. I now need you to go to www.1spark.net and download the One Spark card.

   B. Please COMMIT to doing twenty Sparks. You can use money for ten of them, but for the other ten you can't use anything except your creativity.

   C. Once this is done, I need you to write in the same $1 English composition book that you purchased...OH, I forgot to tell you to purchase the book. Buy an English composition book, and then write down how the Sparks made you feel and how you think they made the people feel that you gave the Sparks to.

   I have written down every Spark that I have ever done. When I'm feeling a little down, all I have to do is read a few of the Sparks that I have completed.

How to Change Your Pickles and Anchors into Keys!

This book will teach you how to turn your
pain into someone else's gain

"I loved reading this book. There is one thing for sure, though. You
are going to need a lot of tissues to get through it!"
– Carma Cryer Harris